Rich Dad's
ADVISORS ™

My poor dad often said, "What you know is important." My rich dad said, "If you want to be rich, *who* you know is more important than *what* you know." Rich dad explained further, saying, "Business and investing is a team sport. The average investor or small-business person loses financially because they do not have a team. Instead of a team, they act as individuals who are trampled by very smart teams." That is why the Rich Dad's Advisors book series was born. Rich Dad's Advisors will guide you to help you know who to look for and what questions to ask of your advisors so you can go out and gather your own great team of advisors.

Robert T. Kiyosaki

Author of the *New York Times* Bestsellers
Rich Dad Poor Dad™
Rich Dad's CASHFLOW Quadrant™
Rich Dad's Guide to Investing™
and *Rich Dad's Rich Kid Smart Kid*™

Rich Dad's™ *Classics*

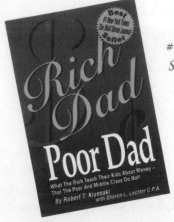

#1 *New York Times*, #1 *Wall Street Journal*, #1 *Business Week*, #1 *Publishers Weekly*, as well as a *San Francisco Chronicle* and *USA Today* bestseller. Also featured on the bestseller lists of Amazon.com, Amazon.com UK and Germany, E-trade.com, *Sydney Morning Herald* (Australia), *Sun Herald* (Australia), *Business Review Weekly* (Australia), Borders Books and Music (U.S. and Singapore), and Barnes & Noble.com.

Wall Street Journal, New York Times business and *Business Week* bestseller. Also featured on the bestseller lists of the *Sydney Morning Herald* (Australia), *Sun Herald* (Australia), *Business Review Weekly* (Australia), and Amazon.com, Barnes & Noble.com, Borders Books and Music (U.S. and Singapore).

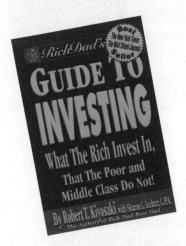

USA Today, Wall Street Journal, New York Times business, *Business Week*, and *Publishers Weekly* bestseller.

Wall Street Journal, New York Times, and *USA Today* bestseller.

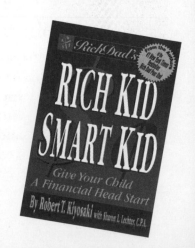

Rich Dad's Advisors™ Series

Rich Dad said,
"Business and Investing is a team sport."

Each of us has a million-dollar idea in our head. The first step in turning your idea into millions, maybe even billions of dollars, is to protect that idea. Michael Lechter is an internationally known intellectual property attorney who is Robert Kiyosaki's legal advisor on all his intellectual property matters. His book is simply written and is an important addition to any businessperson's library.

Loopholes of the Rich is for the aspiring as well as the advanced business owner who is looking for better and smarter ways to legally pay less tax and protect his or her assets. It gives real solutions that will be easy to apply to your unique situation. Diane Kennedy offers over twenty years of experience in research, application, and creation of innovative tax solutions and is Robert Kiyosaki's personal and corporate tax strategist.

Your most important skill in business is your ability to communicate and sell! SalesDogs™ is a highly educational, inspirational, and somewhat "irreverent" look at the world of sales, communications, and the different characters that occupy that world. All of us sell in one way or another. It is important for you to find your own unique style. Blair Singer is respected internationally as an extraordinary trainer, speaker, and consultant in the fields of sales, communication, and management.

Rich Dad's
ADVISORS™

$ales Dogs®

You do not have to be an attack dog to be successful in sales

---

BLAIR SINGER
SALES COMMUNICATION SPECIALIST

WARNER
BUSINESS
BOOKS™

Published by Warner Books

An AOL Time Warner Company

Published by Warner Books in association with CASHFLOW Technologies, Inc., and BI Capital, Inc.

CASHFLOW, Rich Dad, and Rich Dad's Advisors are trademarks of CASHFLOW Technologies, Inc. SalesDogs is a registered trademark of XCEL Training, Inc.

 is a trademark of
CASHFLOW Technologies, Inc.

 Warner Business Books are published by Warner Books, Inc.,
1271 Avenue of the Americas, New York, NY 10020

Visit our Web site at www.twbookmark.com.

For information on Time Warner Trade Publishing's online program, visit www.ipublish.com.

 An AOL Time Warner Company

The Warner Business Book logo is a trademark of Warner Books, Inc.

Printed in the United States of America

First Printing: June 2001
10 9 8 7 6 5 4 3

LCCN: 2001087326
ISBN: 0-446-67833-3

Designed by imagesupport.com, LLC

Book design by Stanley S. Drate / Folio Graphics Co. Inc.

*This book is dedicated to all the lonely
sales managers throughout time
who ever tried to teach their
"old dogs some new tricks"!*

To my son Benjamin, who is the Ultimate SalesDog!

Acknowledgments

I can only say that I have been blessed in my life to have been in the presence of the best teachers and leaders there have ever been. You may not read about them in *Fortune* magazine and they may not have ended up in a history book or in *Who's Who*, but my life is rich today because of them. It seems that they have always presented themselves to me, as Dr. Buckminster Fuller once said, "Always and only in the nick of time!" I only hope that the lessons passed on to me will benefit others in ways that will honor my teachers.

Some of the people and teachers who have inspired and supported me are Eileen, my wife, who has always supported me and taught me the true meaning of unconditional love. My son Benjamin, who is the most wondrous inspiration ever created. My dear friend Robert Kiyosaki, whose brilliant mind helped create this project and without whom I might still be wondering who I could be someday. Kim Kiyosaki, who has always been a shining light and a wealth of informational and personal support. My father and grandfather, who are and were the greatest SalesDogs of all time. They taught me courage, integrity, humor and persistence. My mother and my grandmother, who showed me that strength is found in the power of love and commitment. My brother and two sisters, who have always been my best friends and my best sounding boards. My great late business mentor Robert Etelson, without whom I might still be driving a tractor in Ohio.

Thank you to my friend David Avrick, who has never refused to offer great mentoring advice, and to the incredible friends who have supported me in making this possible: Wayne and Lynn Morgan, Keith Cunningham (the ultimate Big Dog), Herman Wright (the Champion SalesDog), Richard and Veronica Tan, P. J. Johnston and Suzi Dafnis, Paul and Wendy Buckingham, Carol Lacey, Lawrence West, Jayne-Taylor Johnson, Pauline Abel, for her ability to keep me organized, Brenda Saunders, Jamie Danforth, Julie Belden, Dianne Coles, Sherry Maysonave, Cheri Clark, D. C. Harrison, and all of those many people who entrusted a piece of their precious time and education to me over the years.

A very special acknowledgment to the writing talents of Karen McCreadie from "Aussieland," who was able to make *SalesDogs* readable and understandable and who was finally able to interpret what I have been trying to say for years. And to Mike Reynolds and his team for website design and input to the book.

And of course to Einstein's brilliant combination of art, humor and creativity, which gave *SalesDogs* life, form and its irreverent spirit.

Contents

Foreword

My rich dad said,

"Your *wealth,* your *power,* and your *happiness* improve
with your ability to communicate."

—*Robert Kiyosaki*

Poor Dad's Advice

When I returned from the war in Vietnam, it was time for me
to make up my mind whose advice I was going to follow. Was I
going to follow in my rich dad's footsteps or my poor dad's? My
real dad said, "You should go back to school and get your master's degree." When I asked him why, he said, "So you can get
a higher GS rating and higher pay." I then asked him, "What is
a GS rating?"

My dad went on to explain that *GS* stood for "government
service" and that a higher academic degree helped in a higher
GS rating, which meant higher pay. I was still in the U.S. Marine Corps, and the idea of going from one government institution to another government institution was *not* high on my
agenda. I liked the Marine Corps, but I did not like the way the
government promoted by seniority, formal education, tenure
and other factors out of an individual's control. I had seen too

many incompetent officers get promoted over their more competent peers just because they were great "yes men," not great leaders.

My dad's advice to go back to school only to reenter government service at a higher pay scale did not excite me. I was looking for an opportunity to get ahead based upon my *financial results*, rather than my *academic results* and my government pay scale. I definitely did not want to spend the rest of my life employed by a system that told me how much I could earn, what my benefits were, who was senior to me, when I could retire and how much I would make after I retired.

Rich Dad's Advice

When I told my rich dad that I had decided to follow in his footsteps and enter the world of business, he *did not* encourage me to go back to school. Instead he said, "If you want to enter the world of business, you must first learn how to sell."

"Learn to sell?" I said. "But I want to be an entrepreneur. I want to be like you. I want to own large businesses and have lots of people working for me. I want to invest in real estate, and own land and large buildings. I don't want to be a salesman."

Rich dad just laughed at my naïveté.

"Why are you laughing?" I asked. "What does selling have to do with building businesses, managing people, raising money and investing?"

Again rich dad just laughed and said, "Everything."

A Change of Attitude

In *Rich Dad Poor Dad,* readers will have learned that I grew up in a family of educators. It was expected that we would all go on for our master's degrees and even our doctorate degrees.

While high academic degrees were held in high esteem, at the other end of the spectrum was the salesman. In my family of intellectuals, salesmen were found at the bottom of the totem pole. When my rich dad informed me that my first step in entering the business world was to become a salesman, my family's revulsion toward salesmen jumped to life in my body, mind and soul. If I were going to follow my rich dad's advice, I needed to have a radical change in my attitude toward selling and becoming a salesperson.

Tin Men

A number of years ago Hollywood put out a movie, *Tin Men*. It was about salesmen who went door to door selling aluminum siding for houses. As I watched the movie I found it difficult to laugh, even though it was a very funny movie. I could not laugh simply because the movie was real life.

While I was in high school my mom and dad let two "tin men" into the house. These two men sat with my mom and dad at the kitchen table and began their sales pitch. About an hour later the two salesmen had a signed contract. As my mom wrote a deposit check, one of the salesmen stood up, shook hands with my parents and went down to his car. The sale had been made.

The next thing we all heard was the sound of the ripping and cracking of wood. Mom, Dad, the salesman, my brother and I ran out the door and down the stairs. Standing at the foot of the stairs was the tin man who had gone to the car. He had taken a crowbar from his trunk and was now using it to rip off a side of our house.

My mom and dad were speechless. Their faces showed absolute shock and disbelief. "What are you doing?" my dad finally asked.

"Don't you worry, Mr. Kiyosaki," said the tin man holding the crowbar. "We're just beginning our work."

The second tin man went to the car and got out a section of aluminum siding, and both men hammered it over the broken section of our house. "There," said one of the tin men. "The work has begun. When we receive the balance of your payment, we will be back to finish the job." With that, both men hopped in their car and drove off.

For months that corner of our house remained broken and exposed, with a ragged piece of aluminum siding tacked to it. My mom and dad were very upset, they argued and lost sleep for months as they tried to get out of the contract and get their money back. They demanded that the corner of our house be fixed. I remember my mom saying to me, "If your father has a heart attack and dies because of what these two salesman are putting him through, I will never forgive them." I too was very concerned about my dad's health.

The tin men never came back. After six months of heated phone calls, the aluminum siding company finally returned their contract with a *canceled* stamp across the front of it. Although my parents were let out of the contract, the company refused to return the deposit or fix the corner of our house where the aluminum siding hung. So the battle continued. After months of staring at the grim reminder of the incident, our next-door neighbor came over, took down the siding and repaired the damage done by the crowbar. From then on all my parents could say about *all* salesmen was that *all* salesmen were scum, crooks, lazy, liars, unethical, opportunists, bums and other such descriptive adjectives.

Some ten years after the tin men event, my rich dad was advising me to learn to become a professional salesman. As rich dad was talking to me, the only thing going through my head was "How am I going to tell Dad that I am going to learn to be a tin man?"

Some of the Best Advice I Ever Had

When young people ask me what they should do to begin their business career, I offer them the same advice my rich dad offered me. I advise them to get a job in *sales*. I tell them that my rich dad's advice to get a job that had a formal sales training program was some of the best advice I ever had.

Instead of these young people seeing the wisdom in that advice, I often get back the same response I gave my rich dad years ago. The response that goes "But I have a college degree. Shouldn't I start in management . . . not sales?"

When this happens, I tell them the tin man story and add my rich dad's point of view on tin men. In regards to tin men, my rich dad said, "The world is filled with tin men. They can be found in all professions, not just sales. There are tin men in education, medicine, law, politics and religion, so do not evaluate the profession of sales based on your experience with a few tin men. Tin men are tin men because they are *not* good salespeople. Manipulation, deception, pressure, false sincerity, phony smiles, is *not* selling. *Selling is communication.* True selling is caring, listening, solving problems and serving your fellow human being."

To rich dad, selling meant being able to overcome our personal doubts, fears and wants, and going out day after day with only the idea of serving our fellow human beings. To him that was what selling was about. He said, "True selling or communication is not about how many sales you make or how big your commission check is. True selling means being *passionate* about your company's product or service and being *compassionate* with the wants, dreams and needs of your fellow human beings."

Rich dad believed in the law of reciprocity—that is, the Golden Rule. He knew that your sales ability was not only measured by the size of your commission check. Instead he said, "Keep improving your ability to sell and to communicate, and your life will improve if you use your skill to help other people." He continually emphasized that point by saying, "Your *wealth*, your *power* and your *happiness* improve with your ability to communicate. It is your most important skill in the world of business and in life. Keep improving your communication skills, use your skills to improve the lives of others, and your life will also improve."

No matter what business you choose, the ability to communicate and sell is essential to your success.

Great Leaders Are Great Communicators

The clincher for me, in deciding to enter the world of sales, was rich dad pointing out that great leaders were great communicators. Rich dad reminded me of the power of Lincoln's Gettysburg Address. Rich dad said, "That man sold the idea that a war was worth the cause it was being fought for." Rich dad pointed out the power of John F. Kennedy's speech selling the idea that we would put a human being on the moon. Being a very religious man, rich dad also pointed out the quiet power of people like Mother Teresa, selling the reminder of our need to be compassionate human beings.

Rich dad said, "If you have dreams of someday becoming a great leader in whatever field you choose, continually work on improving your ability to sell, for that is what makes a leader great. It is his or her ability to sell an idea that changes lives and history forever."

Sales Training Begins

In 1974 I left the U.S. Marine Corps and joined the Xerox Corporation. I joined Xerox because it had an excellent sales training program. In fact, it is a program that they market to other companies. Yet as good as the sales training program was, the real lessons began in the sales office and on the streets.

Learning to sell was, for me, one of the hardest things I had to do. Being very shy and introverted, the terror I went through each time I knocked on a door was worse than the terror I felt in Vietnam. I hated the fear and nausea I went through each morning for two years. I hated telling my sales manager that I had another bad month without any sales. I hated looking at my commission check and realizing that I might not be able to pay my bills that month. I hated everything about learning to sell—yet it was the best business training I could have gone through. I can honestly say that my wealth, power and happiness today are directly linked to my ability to sell and to communicate.

Why SalesDogs™ Is Important

Blair Singer has been one of my very best friends for over twenty years. He is a great communicator, a great teacher and a great human being. His book *SalesDogs* brings a bit of humor to this often dry and serious subject. When Blair and I first began discussing his book in 1999, we both went back to our memories of being new salesmen, sitting in the sales conference room filled with all types of salespeople. We laughed and joked about the cast of characters that sat in that room every Monday morning, waiting for the pep talk from our sales manager. That was when Blair made the comment, "Trying to train a room full of salespeople was worse than trying to train a room full of dogs." That was when he introduced the idea that the sales department of a business was really a dog kennel, filled with mutts and pedigrees of many different breeds. The SalesDogs™ training program was born.

I am proud to have Blair Singer as a Rich Dad's Advisor, and his *SalesDogs* book as part of the Rich Dad's Advisors Series. If rich dad were alive today, he would also be very proud and happy. If he were here now, my rich dad would say to you, "Keep improving your ability to sell and to communicate. Your *wealth*, your *power* and your *happiness* improve with your ability to communicate."

Please read, enjoy and learn from this book. Then go forth and prosper.

—Robert Kiyosaki

AUDIO DOWNLOAD

In each of our books we like to provide an audio interview as a bonus with additional insights. As a thank-you to you for reading this book, you may go to the Web site www.richdad.com/advisors.

Thank you for your interest in your financial education.

Introduction

In Robert Kiyosaki's *CASHFLOW Quadrant*, he refers to the E (employee), S (self-employed), B (business owner) and I (investor) categories. It is certainly true that the greatest opportunities to amass wealth come from the B/I side of things. Yet one of the largest stumbling blocks that keep people from succeeding in business or even attempting to build a business is their fear or dislike of sales or their inability to sell. If you cannot sell, you cannot build a business. Sales and leadership go hand in hand, as both are concerned with delivering a vision of something better and convincing others to agree and act on that vision. I have never seen a great leader who could not sell, persuade or influence.

For those that are not yet ready for the B quadrant or who simply do not want to go there, the next greatest potential for generating income is by learning to sell. With that tool in your possession, you can speed your way to the B or the I quadrant by accumulating great income from sales through commissions, royalties, equity and bonuses. You can gain way more than someone else who is locked into a fixed paycheck. Rather than begging for a raise, which puts you at the mercy of someone else, you can simply go out and sell more.

My dad (not rich or poor) and my grandfather gave me a great gift. It was the gift of knowing that I could create income anytime, anyplace, anywhere. They taught me that if I could provide a product, service or opportunity that filled or exceeded another's needs, I could always make money. All I had to do was be able to sell it!

If you have any intention of succeeding on the B side of things, you must become a SalesDog. If not, you will have great dreams but no results.

SalesDogs was written because I have been in and around this profession for over thirty years and I have seen firsthand the incredible successes as well as the frustrations of people in sales all over the world. The lows can be minimized and the highs accelerated by simply examining a few basic beliefs about selling and influencing others.

I also own a dog. And over the years I have noticed the striking similarities between our canine friends and us. There is no greater companion in the world than "man's best friend." Dogs throughout the ages have defended their masters, tracked down food for feasts and offered love and friendship when all others have long gone. They are unflappable, unstoppable, eternally optimistic and persistent to the end—just like any great salesperson.

By the end of this book, if you read it, learn it and implement its lessons, one of four things will happen.

1. If you already love sales your income will go through the roof.
2. If you're not that proud that you are in sales you'll be puffed up like a peacock and raring to go.
3. If you are not in sales you'll either want to consider getting in or you will relook at how powerfully you can affect the world around you.
4. You'll want to buy a dog!

Business today judges us by who can generate the most interest, excitement and commitment toward his or her respective service, product, opportunity or point of view. And while some people yield fantastic dollars, others languish in mediocrity.

What's the difference? How do you become the winner in the battle for other people's energy, commitment, time and money?

The answer is within each of us in the form of natural TALENT and learned SKILL. Those that have the most talent *and* skill to enroll others and generate the most influence will make the most sales and the most income.

In order to do that we need to dispel a few sales myths once and for all . . .

Myth 1

You have to be an "attack dog" to be successful in the world of sales. Only certain people can "do" sales.

Fact 1

For too long the "key" to sales has been presented as the Holy Grail. Countless books, tapes and gurus all profess to know the secret to sales mastery and success. We have dissected, analyzed, systematized, jargonized and "purified" sales to the point that we have lost touch with the essence of selling and forgotten the simple truth.

The truth is you don't have to be a thick-skinned "attack dog" to be successful in sales. That is only one type of SalesDog. There are actually five breeds of SalesDogs. If you can discover what breed you are naturally and use that talent, it is then simply a question of playing to your strength. And if you can then go on to learn a few skills from the other breeds you will enjoy even greater success.

For example, a Golden Retriever is the happiest, friendliest, most lovable dog on the planet—he will wag his tail and slobber all over you at every opportunity. BUT if you threaten his master—suddenly he's not so friendly! The Golden Retriever's talent is to be friendly and lovable, but he can be trained with a few Pit Bull skills.

We are all individuals and any effort to pour us all into the set mold of the perfect salesperson is doomed from the start and will do nothing but make the vast majority of us unhappy and spectacularly unsuccessful.

Myth 2

We are told that we have to be "well rounded" enough to master **every** *skill* and possess every *talent* that a salesperson should have. Impossible! That person does not exist! Traditionally we are assessed and told we must strengthen our weaknesses, often forced to struggle and fight against our own nature in a futile attempt to become perfect.

Fact 2

The secret to success does not lie in the formation of "rounded" droids. We don't have to be everything to everyone. We need only be ourselves, understand and accept who we are and use that knowledge to capitalize on our strengths.

Attempting to convert weaknesses into strengths is a waste of time! Finding what you can do WELL and taking full advantage of those strengths is challenging enough!

What if I were to tell you that you are OK just the way you are?

What if I were to tell you that you could make thousands of additional dollars in sales, just the way you are?

What if I were to tell you I could teach you how?

Myth 3

All salespeople are sharks.

There are people out there (Hey, you may be one of them!) who would rank sales below sewerage technician or human guinea pig for nuclear science as their chosen profession or the person they'd most like to meet!

To you guys who hold that view, being "sold" anything, never mind working in sales, is a fate worse than death. And the mere mention of the word conjures up visions of sleazy, cigar-chomping sloths out to take advantage of anyone they can.

Fact 3

First of all, if you fear that you might be viewed this way, or have that vision yourself, it's going to be tough to come across in a credible way. Your fear or dislike of the profession will be reflected in your effectiveness.

Salespeople are simply information gatherers and deliverers of needed services, products and opportunities. You must first transform your view of sales in order to sell. John F. Kennedy sold, Martin Luther King sold, Gandhi sold, your kids are constantly selling. Michael Dell, Lou Gerstner, Warren Buffet, Vince Lombardi, your minister, your parents—they all sell. These folks have all delivered compelling information at critical times to enable others to rise to higher levels of productivity, competency and personal advantage. The image you choose is your own.

Myth 4

I've been in sales my whole life—there's nothing I don't know.

Fact 4

The world we live in today is not the same as the one we lived in yesterday and is different again from the one we'll live in tomorrow. Never in history has change been so rapid. What worked yesterday may not work tomorrow, so the successful SalesDog MUST keep learning to stay ahead of the pack.

SalesDogs teaches a mindset that will give you **the mental and emotional edge to win.** It is an education of skills, techniques and strategies that will accelerate your sales efforts.

And even old SalesDogs can become competitive again—if they are committed to learning and growing. All dogs can hunt—some have just forgotten how because they are overfed and lack exercise. The dogs that can't hunt are simply victims of their own ego and lack of desire to keep learning, growing and adopting new skills. Those dogs can't compete anymore with the young pups on the street. To keep up you have to keep learning.

Myth 5

I don't work in sales.

Fact 5

Whether you consider yourself a salesperson or not, the lessons of sales are incredibly valuable. They are the same lessons that will give you whatever it is you want from your life.

I would maintain that everyone sells. If you're married or in a relationship, if you have kids, if you are a business owner, if you are an employee, in fact, if you have a pulse, you are in a high-pitched sales contest most of the time. Life is sales. And the members of your sales team change as you change, depending on the phases of your life and the crisis or situation at hand.

If you work on a team, handling objections and convincing others is a constant process. Dealing with your boss, your banker, your siblings, vendors, collectors and the guy next door are all part of the sales process.

However, *the* most important sales contract that you will ever win is the one with yourself. You are your harshest critic, your most difficult client and your own personal objection/rejection machine. Yet you must sell to yourself on a daily basis.

The skills inherent in sales are probably the most life-changing skills people can have, even if they never call on one prospect. I can tell you that learning and mastering those skills has woven the tapestry of my life. The incredible quality of my marriage, my family, my career, my friends, my lifestyle are a direct result of the lessons I have learned and implemented from sales.

And most of that was not learned from any sales training course or high-priced consultant. It is the result of thirty years of observation, understanding and implementation. The more you review this book, the more it will make your life easier, richer and more rewarding.

SalesDogs takes both a serious and an irreverent view of ourselves. There is a "dog" in each of us. And there is also a jewel. *SalesDogs* is an attempt to teach you to see both.

Through a bit of humor, powerful personal development training, and many breakthrough techniques, *SalesDogs* is designed to elevate you to be as strong as you want to be, solely for the advantage of yourself and others. The more you serve, the more you are rewarded.

SalesDogs will make any type of selling easier. You will learn to recognize yourself for the SalesDog you are so you can leverage your talent into cash. It will also teach you the best sales skills, mental skills and emotional skills from the other breeds so you can enhance your natural talents and be the leader of the pack.

SalesDogs is a methodology that helps you to uncover and capitalize on your strengths.

Sales is a true personal development journey. Everything that you learn about selling, about people, about presenting, about marketing, about handling objections will put cash directly in your pocket. You learn every day about *who you really are* and what you are made of.

What an adventure!

A true SalesDog knows that enthusiasm, energy and good training can only translate into personal satisfaction and cash! This book is your own personal training program toward a richer, happier, more enjoyable life. The more you read it, the more you will sell and the more fun it will become.

So let's go hunting.

Author's Notes

While some of the chapters of this book may seem to address sales managers, the information is actually directed to all salespeople. It will help you, as a salesperson, to recognize your own breed so that you can own your own strengths while giving you the insight to minimize your weaknesses. And if you are a manager it will help you to recognize the breed of your Sales-Dogs so that you can assign the right pooch to the right prey! The insights are equally powerful for both salespeople and managers.

The best SalesDogs of all will do everything they can to learn as much as they can about how to motivate themselves and others.

I also want to officially relinquish any claim to accuracy

about the individual habits and the thinking processes of dogs. I am *not* a dog expert and this book is not based upon scientific studies of dogs. It is based simply upon my amateur experience with dogs and my professional experience with thousands of salespeople. If you are a dog expert, dog-lover or detailaholic, please do not take offense. The purpose of this book is to help you to learn, to have fun and to become as powerful as you can be.

Are You a SalesDog?

The moment is here!

The answer is about to arrive. All of the months of hard work, waiting, wondering and anticipating will be over in a few short minutes.

You live in a unique world of black and white. There is no reward for second place. This is an all-or-nothing game. Winner takes the prize and the loser walks away hungry. Despite the complex and carefully woven language of our profession, there are really only two words that matter—"Yes" and "No."

As you wait for the answer, your mind can't help but play back the tape of the last few months. . . . It all began in a crowded elevator three months ago when a friend handed you a scrap of paper. On the paper was a name and a phone number. "Give them a call," your friend said, "I think they might be interested."

The game was afoot . . .

You made the initial contact—battling your way through a world-class personal assistant to reach your decision-maker. There were meetings. Scores of e-mails were exchanged. The turning point came during a pivotal teleconference call. You piqued their interest and you made it to the final cut.

It was soon time to present. You'd scouted the competition and if all went well, you knew this account was yours for the taking. During the presentation, you were at the top of your game. Your movements were smooth. Your voice carried with power and reason. In a dimly lit room you moved through your presentation with grace and precision. You drove home your point with carefully crafted beams of light. Everything was perfect. Until, that is, you got "The Question."

There was an almost audible gasp as your team heard "The Question," but you stood tall and delivered your response in your trademark unflappable style. It was a tough question, but you were well rehearsed and prepared. No one in the room detected the concern that echoed silently through your mind.

Or did they? Should you have answered the question differently?

These are the ifs, buts and maybes of hindsight; these are the thoughts that plague you as you wait for the jury to return their verdict. There is nothing more you can say, nothing left to add, nothing but the uneasy uncertainty that now fills your mind. All of your efforts hinge on the discussion taking place behind a closed boardroom door on the thirtieth floor of a Manhattan highrise.

You look at the clock and watch the second hand move in triple-slow motion. You are keenly aware that by now hands have been raised. The vote has been tallied and the decision is made.

You're shaken out of your internal movie by the sound of the telephone. You have to stop yourself from falling over the desk as you lunge to answer—you just want to know, the torment is worse than the decision! Just in time you stop yourself, gather your thoughts, put on your poker face, take a deep breath—"Hey if I get it, great; if not, tomorrow's another day." After a couple of rings you pick up the receiver, and with as much optimism as you can muster say . . .

"Hello."

Does this scene sound familiar? It should. We have all been there.

It's life in the trenches. It's a constant, relentless pursuit. There are many losses and rejections sprinkled between the victories. Joy, anticipation, elation and excitement mingle uneasily with fear, rejection and despondency. One minute you feel ten feet tall and bulletproof, the next a klutz! But still, it's the thrill of the chase that keeps drawing us inexplicably back.

Many salespeople will share with each other in private that it's "a dog's life" in the world of sales. However, hidden in the sarcasm is more truth then you might think. As salespeople we have much in common with our canine friends.

For instance, have you ever watched a dog chase a stick?

You pick up the stick and hurl it far across a lush, green meadow. With tongue hanging, drool flowing and ears flapping, the dog seems to glide over the daisies and buttercups, all muscles straining, in a relentless pursuit of the stick. A smile pasted from jowl to jowl, the dog's mind dances with excitement, because this moment is heaven. All the pestering to get taken out for a walk, all the whining and scratching, all the effort to get to the park was worth it—the dog lives to chase that stick!

Have you ever asked yourself, "What is it that makes dogs LOVE to chase sticks?"

Have you ever asked yourself, "Why is it that I keep chasing deals?"

If you have ever watched a dog pester someone to toss a ball or a stick to him, you will begin to understand the similarity between sales and dogs. A dog will drop that slobbery stick at that innocent person's feet over and over again. In their own way, they somehow KNOW that the person will eventually pick it up and toss it for them. Despite the many times that the dog is ignored or rejected, he will return with the same enthusiasm and anticipation the next time around.

Kids are the same.

My son Benjamin, when he gets his mind set on doing something, is just as relentless.

"Daddy, will you come play with me?"

"Sure Ben, one second until I finish typing this."

"Daddy, will you come play with me now?"

"Sure Ben, I said just one minute."

"Daddy, is a minute up yet?"

If you have ever asked, ever begged, ever tried to convince, negotiate, maneuver or even manipulate another person's point of view, you are in sales. In fact, if you really enjoy winning these types of situations, you may have more in common with our canine friend than you think and possibly even more to learn from him. You may be what I call a "SalesDog"!

The truth is that a SalesDog's life is a great life.

The champion SalesDogs of the world are among the most respected, highly paid and sought-after corporate heroes of our time. Without SalesDogs, businesses cannot survive. Without *great* SalesDogs, businesses cannot thrive. Nearly all great business leaders, successful entrepreneurs and great investors trace their roots and the core of their success to their sales training and sales experience.

The ability to fetch and to hunt with passion, talent and skill is a unique and treasured gift. Without question, the better you are at selling or convincing or negotiating, the more of the world is open to you in terms of wealth, opportunities and great relationships.

The rewards of large inflows of cash commissions, ever-expanding networks, resounding accolades and free and unencumbered lifestyle are available to anyone, whether you are meek and quiet, social and friendly or even technical and intellectual, and whether you are in corporate sales, network marketing or independent sales like real estate, or in insurance or retail.

The key to success is not trying to copy the traits of others, but learning how to leverage your own unique talents. So first you must identify your breed. In the following chapters we will highlight the characteristics of each pooch.

Once you know what breed of SalesDog you are, you can generate hundreds of thousands of dollars in cash to build the lifestyle that you want. You can learn what your natural strengths are so that you can turn them into positive results for yourself. You can also spot your natural soft spots and learn how to avoid them or compensate for them so that you can generate "yeses" everywhere in your life. If you choose to learn the ways of the great SalesDogs, you can have whatever wealth you desire.

And since sales can be a team sport, your ability to identify the talents and breeds of those around you will have a tremendous impact on your chances of success. Everyone who is in contact with your prospects is part of your team. Whether you are a sales manager or a member of the sales team, being able to identify the breeds of your colleagues will be an extremely valuable tool.

You'll learn how to understand those around you and to translate that knowledge into amazing results.

CAUTION: Not everyone is a DOG! This is not about cats, horses or birds. If you are a dog, you may be able to hunt. I cannot speak for other species. Deep inside, do you suspect a bit of a canine urge?

Are you still unsure if you are a SalesDog? Ask yourself the following questions:

- Do you get a "rush" when a prospect says "yes" to you?
- Is the "hunt" sometimes better than the reward?
- Would you give up a little commission for additional fame, accolades and recognition?
- Do you have a natural persistent streak in you?
- Do you have a soft spot for a good story?
- Do you have a tendency to try to convince others?
- Do you find that when you are talking in a group about something that you are interested in your voice gets louder and that you naturally get more dramatic?
- Do you experience ranges of emotion from being a legend in your own mind to being a complete klutz?
- Do you have fun occasionally "people watching"?
- Do you spend time trying to figure out other people's psychology?
- Do you love to win?

If you answered "yes" to at least some of these questions, you may be a true-blue SalesDog who has the potential to make tons of money. It is simply a matter of knowing your breed, learning the best of other breeds and following the simple yet powerful example set by that contented canine lounging in the corner of your kitchen right now.

ALL DOGS CAN HUNT and SELL and WIN, yet **some will and some will not.** Are you ready to learn what it takes to "get the stick"?

Let me give you an example of a champion SalesDog. There was no magic, no gimmick, and he was selling a service that had no major bells and whistles over the competition. It's just that he was a SalesDog.

Years ago he was selling health insurance in Austin, Texas. As an account manager he was prospecting for new businesses that needed health insurance for their employees. He happened into a small office in which could be seen about a dozen people scurrying around assembling personal computers. There were tables stacked with circuit boards and boxes lying all around. He asked to see the owner and was directed toward a twenty-year-old sitting at a back table working. It turned out that this young fellow had just left the University of Texas and had decided to build his own company assembling PCs. My friend the SalesDog had a hunch about this guy's vision for the company that he wanted to build. The problem was that the SalesDog's insurance company would not write a policy for a company with less than fifty employees. Our young PC guru had only sixteen. For my friend, the real sales pitch had to begin. He went through his manager, around the organization and everywhere he could to get around this deal-breaking rule. His boss said no, but for a real SalesDog that means go! Through impetuous selling and bending a few rules he was able to secure the business. Within one year this little business went from sixteen employees to a staff of five hundred! That guy behind the table was Michael Dell, and his company is now legendary.

This is a valuable lesson: To be a great SalesDog you sometimes have to jump fences to get to the goal. You have to be willing to bend the rules, to sacrifice a few sacred cows to get the best deals. Many times that means the toughest sell is to your own team or your own company. If it adds value to all concerned and it's legal, ethical and moral, do not cower after the first *no*.

The best part of this story, however, is that my friend lost the business to another large healthcare insurer soon after Dell had grown to five hundred employees. The day he lost it, he started his sales cycle all over again. A true SalesDog never quits. He could not seem to get an appointment or to get the attention of anyone at Dell. He took on the detective hat of the Basset Hound and started researching like crazy. In a Dell annual report, he found the name of a person on Dell's board of directors who was also a senior manager for his company. My friend got on the phone and called his head office to track down this lead. After many calls, letters and attempts, my friend got this manager to agree to give a referral to the key buyer in Dell. Did he get the business? No. The fellow at Dell claimed he was happy and did not want to entertain the idea of switching again. Our SalesDog friend began what would become a long process of building a relationship with this individual. He invited him to benefits and sporting events, and he provided a continuous stream of timely information to this buyer—information that was not necessarily promoting our friend's company but was helpful to the person at Dell in keeping up with the changing demands of the insurance industry in a growing company. He built the frequency that will be referred to later. Agreement after agreement after agreement. Serving, serving and serving some more. He built a truly connected relationship with this fellow, until one day, the competitor faltered. There was a phone call, a few exchanged words, and our SalesDog and his firm were back in. By now Dell had 1,500 employees.

By the time my friend left to go to work as the head of sales and marketing at another healthcare insurer, Dell was up to 15,000 employees. (Nice commission checks!)

My friend learned his Retriever lesson in the end. He said, "There was no way that I would ever lose that account again. I made sure that I peed in every corner of Dell computer to secure that territory." He did not really urinate there, but he did create allies in every department. He made sure that the key people at Dell knew of their new health plan, and he made sure that someone was always going in there to be sure that they understood their benefits, how to process their claims and how to handle any problems that might occur. That was ongoing.

My friend's name is Herman, and he has soared in the arena of healthcare insurance. I asked him if he could summarize the lessons learned. He smiled and said:

1. "Sometimes you have to break the rules." When the company said he could not sell to a company with less than fifty employees, that is when the real selling started. If you are going to serve the customer you have to do the right things!

2. "There is no such thing as a lack of connection." There is always somebody who knows somebody who can get you in the door. If you spend a few hours on the phone, there is no person in the world whom you cannot somehow access through someone else. Look through annual reports, journals, article lists, the Internet, and do your market research!

3. "Your competition's greatest weakness is the day they land a deal." He knew that when he lost that account that was the moment that his competition was feeling the most complacent. They had no idea what he was up to or how he had infiltrated the customer's site with frequency, information and service. When you lose a deal, it only means that a new game has begun.

Why SalesDogs?
(SALESDOGS AND SALESPEOPLE)

It has been said that owners sometimes bear an uncanny resemblance to their dogs. And a quick walk in the park will often prove hilarious testimony to that theory. This becomes really scary when you start to talk to some of these faithful owners and discover that the similarities go way beyond the baggy jowls of the Bulldog or the perked-up nose of the Pekinese.

I am not sure whether the dog takes on the personality of the owner or the owner takes on the personality of the dog. Perhaps each has some "animal" attraction for the other—like the control- and order-orientated macho guys who attract close-cropped intense Dobermans or the drooling cuddly Golden Retriever who attracts the lovable do-anything-for-anyone owners. Whatever the reason, I am sure that somewhere in the world, a team of animal and human behaviorists is feverishly seeking clinical proof of this theory. But the truth is, it doesn't matter much. What is clear is that you can often understand a great deal about a dog simply by understanding the breed, as each has very specific personalities and traits.

DOGS TEND TO LOOK A LOT LIKE THEIR OWNERS

And there is a large solid-gold bone to be unearthed and enjoyed for the salesperson, sales manager, business owner, entrepreneur or network marketer who understands those traits. Understand the dynamics of the canine world and you too could be selling with the precision and tenacity of a HOT dog on the hunt.

The greatest single mistake that salespeople or sales managers make is believing there is one particular set of characteristics or traits that all salespeople need to have to be successful. Their frantic, misguided search for this Holy Grail of sales success often leads them on a path of frustration and envy.

While striving to better ourselves is a noble and much-needed pursuit, attempting to mirror the traits of the "perfect salesperson" is futile and spirit-crushing. Instead, learn to access and develop the "great salesperson" within. Salespeople and sales managers need to identify and understand first their own breed and then the breeds of those around them. With this knowledge, they can leverage their own strengths and personalities and those of their team. That way the manager can send the right pooch to hunt the right prey.

For example, you wouldn't put your money on the Saint Bernard in a Greyhound race. But if you were stranded on a mountainside freezing your butt off—who would you rather see? You need to put yourself, and the members of your sales team, in roles within the sales process that they were born to play.

Many people will find the comparison between salespeople and dogs outright offensive. However, I say that anyone who has figured out how to make big dollars by peddling or selling something is, at some level, a dog. Salespeople seem to have this knack of always coming back for more and never yielding to adversity.

Think about it . . .

- Who is man's best friend?
- What is the most loyal pet you can have?
- Who will defend you to the end?
- What animal will endure just about anything for a pat on the head?
- Who will stick beside you through good times and bad?
- Who looks at you as if you are a god when everyone else thinks you're crazy?
- Who loves you no matter what?
- Who loves to chase a stick?
- Who loves to track down a scent?
- Who can shrug off adversity and come back for more?

You're right! It could be a dog or it could be a salesperson!

I have a friend in Sydney who owns an executive placement firm. (Okay, he is a head-hunter!) He and his partner had been working on landing a huge petrochemical account for many months. They had pitched and presented and presented some more. They had made concessions and accommodations, and though they had been turned back many times and told to "beat it," in true Aussie style they were not about to go down without a fight.

Even when fate turned against them, they kept going. During a presentation to the CEO of the firm, one of them was in the middle of making a dramatic point on a flip chart when one of the legs on the flip chart began to give way. As the flip chart came down, my friend, who was in midsentence and leaning on it, went down with it. Undaunted, he never stopped talking, and even while lying horizontal and still clutching the chart he continued his pitch. There was no giving up. He was like a stubborn dog that was unwilling to be pushed away, told to scram or to give up the stick.

My other friend and the CEO were laughing so hard they never heard the point that he was trying to make so passionately. It was either his tenacity or the comedy that broke the ice, but when he finally got up, the CEO said, "OK, OK, if you want it that bad, you've got it!"

It's simple: Sales are about convincing others to take action on something that they were not necessarily inclined to do beforehand. You could say that the same is true of leadership, parenting, motivating or negotiating. These are all actions that require some sales skills.

Dogs can be great champions, hunters and companions. Yet, as loyal as good dogs can be and as smart as they can be, they require a lot of maintenance. If you are not there to feed them, water them or stroke them regularly, they can get mean or unruly and can even tear up your house when you leave. Salespeople can be the same way if they don't get themselves trained properly.

I have resisted having a dog these last few years because of my incredible travel schedule. It seemed unfair to the dog. Yet, somewhere in the middle of this book, my four-year-old son finally convinced me to get one. I wish I'd owned a dog before I ever tried to direct a group of salespeople! The training is almost the same!

Once properly trained, dogs can hunt with uncanny precision. However, until they are trained, it will require a leash, a lot of patience and usually a plastic glove or a pooper-scooper to clean up after them. Even the good ones will make messes in the beginning. Their early enthusiasm may be difficult to discipline, but if handled well, can yield tons in sales and commissions.

SalesDogs is a unique methodology for understanding the breeds of salespeople. Although it is training philosophy, designed to be entertaining and easy to learn, the concepts behind it are very powerful and are based on many years of research and observation.

What I've discovered through my studies is that there are five breeds of SalesDogs and numerous cross-breed mutts. By comparing and contrasting traits and characteristics of salespeople with those of five distinct breeds of dog, we have an effective and easy-to-learn method for understanding, developing and better motivating our teams.

A true SalesDog knows that education and good training mean both satisfaction and cash. As a SalesDog you must always seek opportunities that provide the best training available . . . not the biggest commission! Many young pups chase the wrong bone.

I went to work at UNISYS years ago because their training was the best in the business. Many of my friends went to companies like XEROX, IBM and AMWAY because in those days, their training was the best. Today they all own their own businesses and are worth millions. When you are taught properly, the money is yours wherever you go!

You will soon learn how to identify the type of dog that you are, the type that you have in your kennel and how to train those dogs to maximize the attributes of their breed.

The first step is to determine your and your team members' innate ability to sell. To save valuable selling time, training resources and disappointment on both sides, there are tools for predicting your success, or the success of your pack, even before the first day of obedience training with the SalesDog Aptitude Test. These will determine if you are in the right mindset to be successful at sales. More about them later.

So what happens if you have the wrong mindset? You can change it as fast as you can test it! Ten minutes of training can make the determination between the ability to sell or not. And with only five skills and four critical mindsets to learn, you will be on your way to sales success and prosperity in no time.

The good news is that almost any dog can hunt, and the processes and procedures for doing that are simple and can generate tons of cash for the smart dog and smart dog trainer.

For those of you who are offended by the prospect of being compared to a dog—the analogy is pure compliment! Sometimes you are a fighter, sometimes you are a lover, and sometimes you are playful and sometimes serene. You live life on the edge, no time to waste (although you may waste it!). You never see two dogs swapping phone numbers—they live for the moment!

Sales is fun, fast and exciting. Think about it. Some salespeople look like dogs, they act like dogs, sometimes after a late night out they may even smell like dogs. Some can track down a prospect like a great hunter and others can flush out and secure even the most elusive of prey.

So what are you?

Identifying the Breed

SalesDog methodology works everywhere where sales are occurring. We sell to our bosses, to our neighbors, and in our relationships on a daily, and even hourly, basis. From questions like "What about a raise?" to "What are we going to watch on television tonight?" there are sales events going on at all times.

While there are more than four hundred different breeds of dog in the world, in the world of sales there are really only five breeds. The question is which one are you? Which one is your boss? If you are a dog trainer (manager), what kind of mongrels do you have in your kennel? If you are a multilevel marketer, which breeds are barking loudest in your downline?

With this in mind, what type of SalesDog have you married? Knowing the answer to that question and how to work it to your favor could be the key to a lifetime of bliss!

Once you are able to identify the breeds in people, the sales game becomes a whole lot easier, and your ability to sniff out the right things to do and say becomes second nature. Knowing your own breed will allow you to immediately leverage your strengths and close more deals. It will give you guidance and wisdom in how you approach the entire sales cycle. Not to mention the peace of mind of just knowing that you can make it to the top just the way you are!

You'll see a change in the way you develop leads, pursue prospects, make presentations and close deals. Rather than learning the "best way," you'll learn the "best way for your breed." You'll also be able to avoid the "dark alleys of sales" where you find yourself on unfamiliar ground and at a disadvantage. You'll be able to stay in control of the environment and always be on your best path.

As a SalesDog or dog trainer, knowing the breed of your prospects will give you an exceptional edge. In hunting, prey for dogs can include ducks, squirrels, bears, Frisbees and tennis balls. For SalesDogs, prey can be large corporations, business owners, your next exceptional distributor, executives and decision-making personal assistants. Different dogs are better at charming different quarry. Putting the right SalesDog on the right job will be critical to your success.

Lapdogs may not be ideally suited for taking on raging bulls, while teeth-baring, saliva-dripping attack dogs may scare the pants off a domestic housewife. What is your target and what is your natural demeanor?

As a SalesDog, sometimes your choice of kennel is limited to those that will take you! Many SalesDogs arrive in their pack through donation, obligation and sometimes by process of elimination. Some have been rescued from the pound and are brought aboard only because someone couldn't resist the sad and pleading eyes of the lonely dog in the window.

Most dog trainers walk into a full kennel when they get started. We adopt (or as some might say, get stuck with) the pack of SalesDogs that we have. Few of us have the luxury (or patience) to recruit and develop our entire sales team from scratch.

Even with those rare times when a SalesDog has been scouted, tested, interviewed and analyzed before being hired, there aren't any sure bets. Some SalesDogs are simply great at testing and at putting on a show in front of the judges. Based on their interview you feel you've snared yourself a blue-ribbon hound. But when it comes time to perform out in the field, you realize you've got nothing but a junkyard dog.

When you first come in, you survey your SalesDogs as they are wandering through the yard. Some are doing fine on their own, while others are languishing—still waiting for a bone. A large number of them may simply be curled up in the corner waiting for something good to happen. Then there are those that are barely hanging on, pleading for a pat on the head and one more chance.

In any case, you don't have to clear the kennel to make progress. If you understand how the different breeds work, you can increase your team's ability to hunt by huge percentages. Yes, you can even turn that old Basset Hound that seems to have lost its scent into a pedigree pooch.

While each pure breed of SalesDog is unique, they do share some common traits. Most are great companions, each offering something special that makes spending time around them enjoyable. Some you like because you're instantly at ease around them, others you are fond of because of their boundless energy. Sometimes SalesDogs can also be a nuisance, especially when they are howling at the moon in triumph, sorrow or longing. Fortunately, a skillfully thrown shoe often solves the problem!

SalesDogs have the ability to make friends easily. There are few people in the world they aren't interested in meeting, except for perhaps other SalesDogs (it's a territorial thing). Because of their canine instincts they have the ability to sniff out deals from places most mortals could never imagine. They can track, sniff, lick, run, bark, whine, yelp and beg. They can also be your greatest friend in times of need.

In the world of the SalesDog there are only five pedigree breeds—Pit Bull, Golden Retriever, Poodle, Chihuahua and Basset Hound.

But there is also a range of cross-breeds—so which one are you? Read on to find out the traits and characteristics of each breed.

Pit Bull

The most aggressive and probably the most stereotyped salesperson is the Pit Bull (this breed is mostly responsible for people's acquired distaste of used-car lots!). Yes, you know them: They will attack anything that has even the remotest scent of "Eau de Prospect." And they will attack with a ferocity, aggression and tenacity that is both awe-inspiring and terrifying. All they need is a pants cuff to latch on to and they NEVER let go. It becomes a vicious snarling fight from beginning to end. Water hoses, clubs, even Mace will not deter this dog from landing its target.

If this SalesDog has a characteristic sound, it would be the one that you might hear as you walk home late at night through some dark, littered alleyway deep in the heart of the city. It's that low sinister "GRRRRR" resonating from out of the darkness by the garbage cans, and in a sudden flash you see the yellow eyes lock and load before the attack. That's the Pit Bull and you're dinner!

PIT BULL

I have a friend, John, who is in the competitive arena of business-machine sales in Canada. Years ago as we were driving outside Toronto, we passed a town that had just been devastated by tornadoes. Houses were literally ripped to pieces, cars and trucks tossed aside like toys, trees splintered and snapped, and the trail of destruction stretched as far as you could see. I was actually feeling bad for the poor victims of this rampage when my friend John, who was driving, simply smirked and said in a low breath, "See that? This is what happened to the last person that said 'No' to me!" HE is a PIT BULL.

If a Pit Bull carries a cell phone (which is probably either frequently lost or out of power), it is only so that he can call as many prospects as he can while driving from point A to point B.

You have to keep throwing Pit Bulls meat, but there is no need for prime rib! Dangle it in front of them, whip them into a frenzy and toss it into the market. They will turn up something for sure. Rest assured, however, that you will receive calls from terrorized prospects and neighbors and may even be asked by authorities to restrain this beast under penalty of law. DO NOT send them to cocktail parties without muzzles, choker chains and sedatives. On second thought, send them to a pub . . . not a cocktail party. There are two essential tools required when training a Pit Bull—raw meat and a stun gun.

The Pit Bull's success comes from sheer power and fearlessness. They will make more calls, field more rejections and keep on selling more than any other breed, even when they should really back off. Adversity is simply a wake-up call. Closing and objection-handling is breakfast for this champion.

However, you will need to keep a close eye on their territory. What they make up for in aggressiveness, they may lack in tactfulness and strategy. Pit Bulls can be very rich or very frustrated, and training is the key.

Golden Retriever

The next breed is everyone's favorite, the Golden Retriever. These slobbering, goo-goo-eyed, shaggy balls of love will do anything for someone who is willing to pet them. They will jump into freezing rivers after rotten sticks, play center field for your son's softball team and, yes, it is advertised that they can even retrieve a beer from the refrigerator.

They are the salespeople who sit attentively panting with big smiles on their jowls waiting for the next command from their prospects. They will sit there with eternal optimism, waiting for the phone to ring, hoping deep inside that their prospect still loves them. They win their clients by racing after anything that the prospect throws to them.

They will fetch any ball, do any favor and bend over backward to please the prospect. They are actually affronted when you talk in terms of "sales." *To the Retriever, customer service is everything.* They operate on the belief that the more you give prospects, the more they will love you and ultimately the more they will buy. They actually beg for the opportunity to do favors for the customer.

I have a very dear friend who sells real estate in Denver. She

GOLDEN RETRIEVER

is a talented salesperson—smart, extremely thorough and a retriever to the core. When I asked her about the key to great sales she metamorphosed right in front of my eyes. She turned to me with those big brown watery eyes and started talking to me in soft soothing tones. I clearly imagined her voice sounding like the whimper of the Golden Retriever that nuzzles up to you for a pat on the head. She simply said, "You give them whatever they want!"

She was appalled at the "seek and destroy" strategies of the Pit Bull. She was absolutely convinced that if you are nice enough to prospects and continue to retrieve for them the phone will never stop ringing. She could not even consider any other way to sell, nor should she—it worked!

Retrievers always have their cell phones on, battery fully charged, twenty-four hours a day. They even have a few spare batteries, fully charged, littered around—just in case. To them it would be unforgivable to be out of touch with their customer in a time of need.

The Retriever sells through providing extraordinary customer service. (Just make sure that they remember to try to sell something once in a while!) Wise Retrievers are successful because they know that if they continually take care of prospects, clients and members of their team, numbers will grow and grow. Their attention to long-term service fuels their success.

Poodle

On the more sophisticated side of sales, there is the Poodle. They are highly intelligent, albeit a bit highly strung, and very conscious of "looking mah-ve-lous!"

Whether it's reality-based, or only in their heads, these salespeople live and thrive in a world of flash and class. They judge books by their covers and prospects by their cars and spend more time at the mall then they do at their desks.

They wear Italian suits, buffed-out black-capped shoes or stiletto pumps, two-hundred-dollar neckties or expensive pearls and drive the kind of automobiles that valets love to park.

Though they cannot always afford their life of luxury, they see all of their purchases as absolutely necessary tools of the trade. The Poodle will sooner call in sick than have to take public transport or make an appearance on a bad hair day.

The Poodle struts! While other dogs tramp, romp and roll through their territories, the Poodle prances, occasionally flashing its shiny-eyed glance toward you in an unmistakable recognition of class. They are incredibly well-connected and probably have the most extensive and exclusive network of any of the breeds. They know who's who and they want you to know it!

While most dogs bark and whine, the Poodle actually speaks in a classy, distinguished tone. In a gathering of other dogs or prospects, the Poodle can always be found among the tinkling of the wineglasses holding court with comments guaranteed to sparkle with wit, wisdom and even dry humor. They love to speak in front of groups and be the center of attention. Indeed, a Poodle's sales pitch is often delivered with such style and panache that even those without a shred of factual information can sound visionary.

Poodles are smooth operators; they live in the fast lane. Latest trends, newest gadgets and hottest parties are all part of the Poodle lifestyle. If appearance and first impression matter to a prospect, the Poodle is the prize pooch.

This breed of SalesDog is constantly looking for ways to reach the most people in the simplest way. *The Poodle is the Ulti-*

mate Marketing Dog. Their abilities to market and to articulate a message can make Poodles large sums of money.

Poodles are great for selling big-ticket items when they can use their regal bearing to impress clients. Just don't ask them to rescue a fallen duck in the swamp, jump into a cold stream or to be caught dead in a dark alley in an unsavory part of town! They will be socializing in more "civilized" circles.

Because of their trainability and natural desire to be the center of attention, canine Poodles have been a favorite with circuses for centuries. SalesDog Poodles are also the life and soul of the party as well as championship schmoozers. They've graduated from high school with titles of "most attractive" or "most popular." Some of them have even maneuvered their way into earning the "most likely to succeed" designation.

I had a friend in Tucson whom I would run across at sales retreats around the country. He drove a 911 Targa, got courtside seats for his best clients to Phoenix Suns basketball games, wore that season's Zegna suits and claimed to have a small harem of women swooning after him. (This proved to be quite an exaggeration—as Poodles are wont to do.)

Despite having zero sleep the night before, and still challenged by a wine-induced hangover, he would prance into the branch office looking impeccable. Prospects loved him and

POODLE

loved to be associated with him. And for him, there was never a shortage of prospects. He was always working hundreds of schemes simultaneously that were skillfully funneling large numbers into his lair.

The guy was definitely a legend in his own mind, and his power of persuasion was impressive. Once, during a sales conference in Chicago, he convinced me to join him for a "night to remember" on the town. I knew better but went anyway.

It was a night to remember all right. I dropped a couple hundred bucks on alcohol and barely made it back to the conference for opening the next morning. I was a wreck. He looked like he just stepped out of a James Bond movie. If he was 007, I was Inspector Clouseau.

Poodles are born with cell phones in their hands. They rely on them to always know what's "happening." Besides, for Poodles, having at least one cell phone in their ear is an important symbol of success.

Chihuahua

The Chihuahua adds a whole new dimension to the sales kennel. This breed's contribution to sales must never be underestimated. Whatever you do, do not be fooled by their small size.

These SalesDogs are usually incredibly bright. Those who own these pocket rockets love them. They are technical wizards and are probably the most intense of all the breeds.

Chihuahua SalesDogs have to be careful when they get excited because unchecked they may talk continuously, and their high-pitched "yipping" can give everyone a headache. These SalesDogs can look as though they are running on too much adrenaline, caffeine or hard-core truck speed.

Chihuahuas are often highly strung, simply because their

bodies are so small and they have so much going on in their brains. They don't usually make the best lapdogs. They aren't that great for cuddling up to, and aren't known for slick people skills, but their passion, product knowledge and understanding of processes are unrivaled.

These wired and hyperactive individuals are merciless in the pursuit of knowledge. Their buggy eyes tell the story of their fanatic approach to research. Chihuahuas can pull off all-nighters better than any other breed. While the rest of the kennel are curled up asleep, the Chihuahua is flitting from website to website, page after page of annual reports, compiling enough data, statistics and information to answer every conceivable objection known to man.

While some of the other breeds need physical exercise to remain healthy, Chihuahuas need mental exercise. Their brainpower is amazing.

By the way, don't make the mistake of getting Chihuahuas started on a subject that they are passionate about. They will ramble on endlessly. As a matter of fact, they won't just talk, they will shout, scream, rant and rave a mile a minute. Prospects can't help but be bowled over by the incredible exhibition of passion, intellect and an arsenal of irrefutable evidence. Even when they haven't a clue what the Chihuahua is talking about!

Years ago at Unisys, I made good friends with a Chihuahua named Brian. As long as you kept him fueled up with pizza and Cokes, he would relentlessly research anything. I can vividly recall collaborating with him on preparing for a computer demo for a prospect. I faded out at 10:00 P.M. and went home. Brian was starting to peak. He labored away the entire night, and in the process discovered new features of the program that even the developers didn't know were possible.

The next morning at the demo (he simply went into the rest room to brush his teeth before we started) he dazzled the

CHIHUAHUA

prospect's technical assistant (another Chihuahua with glasses) with a salvo of bits, bytes, rams and technical goo-gah. He was yipping so fast that both the decision-maker and myself were not only lost but also developing a migraine. We snuck out for a cup of coffee and left the two Chihuahuas yapping away. Two hours later, they were still going at it. The end result of this mad exchange of data and technical tidbits was that our Chihuahua had impressed them enough to earn their confidence in our ability to deliver.

While the Pit Bulls may establish the initial contact, and the Poodles will present the flash, the Chihuahuas are absolutely essential for delivering the proof.

The founder of one of the most wildly successful overseas real-estate companies I have ever encountered is a true success story. His staff swears him to be a full-blown Chihuahua. His intelligence is second to none. He knows the market inside and out. His passion is boundless. In a recent sales conference with his five hundred agents, he stepped up to the stage to give a five-minute introduction. Thirty minutes later he had worked himself into such a passionate frenzy that the whole room was stunned.

It seemed that he never took a breath, yet when he finished you could have heard a pin drop. I could not tell what he said because he went so fast and furiously, but I was definitely inspired. He inspires on pure passion alone!

Beware if you have Chihuahuas on staff. They are very bright, but (probably due to the caffeine and lack of sleep) they can be very emotional and sometimes paranoid if not handled carefully. Mellow is not in their vocabulary. While other breeds might have the latest sporting equipment or fashion, the Chihuahua will almost always have the latest electronic equipment, like a wireless palmtop computer that allows them to data dump from anywhere.

I, for one, have never been one to feel like cuddling a Chihuahua. But I respect them and understand they are absolutely essential to more sophisticated sales cycles.

Basset Hound

The classic of all classics is the faithful old Basset Hound. With his wrinkled brow and drooping ears the Basset is hard to resist.

SalesDog Bassets are like their low-slung counterparts, in personality if not in looks. This sad-eyed companion will stick by you through thick and thin. You could try to chase this dog away, scold and threaten him, but he'd just roll over and take it. Minutes later he'd come cowering back looking at you with those droopy eyes asking for forgiveness. Bassets are never ruffled, never stressed; they are constant and dependable.

I poke particular fun at the Basset Hound because it is the breed I identify with the most. These SalesDogs do not seem to have a lot of class or polish and seldom seem to exude much passion or confidence. But of all the breeds, their ability to build strong, loyal and long-term relationships through sheer strength of personality and personal rapport is amazing.

This breed rarely spends more energy than it needs to. Basset Hounds do not bark often, but they whine and howl a lot. This is especially true when begging—which is their specialty!

Regardless of how old Basset Hounds are, they always look middle-aged. Exercise takes too much effort, so their soft bodies often take the shape of bowling pins. They are the most frumpish of the breeds, and don't have time or ambition to worry about fashion trends.

Their car and desk are littered with debris—old business cards and worn-out leads. This SalesDog is always looking for a bone, but is happy to be graced with even the tiniest of scraps from the table. When they sell, they have that distinctively humble, sometimes groveling approach that is genetically designed to drive an arrow of sympathy deep into your heart. If their pathetic look doesn't get you and begging doesn't work . . . beware! You may be about to experience Plan B—from their wallet, an accordion full of family pictures will drop to the ground, and you'll hear tales of braces, bicycles and unpaid bills. They will stop at nothing to solicit a scrap of sympathy.

Their tenacity is rivaled only by that of the Pit Bull, and this persistence is their strong suit. They are never deterred by rejection, unanswered phone calls and slammed doors. There is no quit in this breed. Their ability to persist, pester, cajole or even beg is legendary and has been known to break down even the stiffest of objections. "Okay, okay! Anything to get you off of my back," cries the prospect. "Where do I sign?"

Mistreated Basset Hounds are not shy about whining about why the world has treated them so unfairly. Just seeing them round the corner and heading toward you in the hallway is enough to make you cringe at times, but don't be misled. Basset Hounds are powerful allies. They can be extremely loyal to their masters, as well as to their prospects and clients. This rapport-building talent and trustworthy demeanor can win Basset Hounds huge dollars over the course of time.

Don't ever expect Poodles to hang out with the Hounds. Simply being seen in public with the Basset would threaten the Poodle's image.

In regard to cell phones, they may tell you that they cannot afford them. And then you'll hear about their kids, the cost of summer camps, crime in the city, ballet classes and the cars breaking down . . .

Despite the lugubrious-faced Basset Hounds' looks, they are incredible tracking and hunting dogs. They have been known to track even the faintest scent over miles of difficult terrain.

Basset Hound

Their amazing ability to follow a scent combined with their intense "look you in the eye" approach makes them a valuable member of the kennel. Never underestimate the kicked-back appearance of your Basset Hound SalesDogs. They have incredible ability to sniff out deals and to win hearts where no one else can.

4

Big Dogs

And then there is the Big Dog!

In the world of SalesDogs, there exists a unique category of dog that roams the kennel with a distinct swagger. Big Dog is not a breed but a state of mind! It only takes one Big Deal to create a Big Dog.

Imagine John Wayne or Clint Eastwood with four paws and a tail, and you have your Big Dog. A bold, brash gambler, Big Dog is a legend in his own lunchtime. Yet it is that same bravado and total self-belief that keep the Big Dog alive during the dry spells—which can be very dry and very long. Unlike his other canine chums who can survive on scraps, Big Dog only eats prime rib. He wouldn't be seen dead scurrying around a dumpster even if his life depended on it.

The Big Dogs roam only where the stage is large, the lights are bright and the crowd is packed to the rafters. They don't bother with multilevel selling unless they can start at the top, because they only have time for the main decision-makers.

They don't have any trouble getting past personal assistants and manage to get even the busiest prospects to return their calls promptly.

They don't hunt for squirrel or pheasant; their eyes are always fixed on the eight-hundred-pound brown bear. It may take a while for them to track one down, but when they do they will snare it with the power and glory that is Big Dogs' trademark. The bloodier the battle, the better the tale, as the story is then retold again and again in full Technicolor to legions of awestruck pups!

When I asked a Big Dog friend of mine whether it was important to sell up through an organization and obtain consensus along the way, he chuckled, and with a low growl said, "That would be a colossal waste of time—find the 'man,' set up the meeting and do the deal!" That was his strategy. I can tell you that his motto is: If you are going to go down—make it big! If you go broke, you don't want to do it over a duplex!

Always aware of creating their legacy, Big Dogs are constantly working on developing tales of their conquests. And they are never shy about embellishing the story as it gets retold. In fact, if exaggeration were an Olympic event, Big Dog would represent her country.

Big Dogs have no patience for nurturing long sales cycles. They are closers and want to get in when the prospect is paying attention, the pen is ready and the inkwell is full.

The great victories provide their moment in the sun and they will bask there for an interminable length of time. As for the crushing defeats, don't expect to get much of an apology from your Big Dogs, because according to them, it is RARELY their fault. They'll say management is just too dumb to understand their vision, and their subordinates are too incompetent to implement their strategies.

The problem with Big Dogs is that their propensity for exaggeration and ferocity can lead to big mistakes—such as misrepresenting the product, completely upsetting the client or infuriating the product development team by promising the prospect that the new state-of-the-art computer system also comes with a voice-activated coffee maker and moonboots.

It's Big Deal or No Deal for the Big Dog, and that mantra also leads to Big Mistakes. Send a Big Dog out for the newspaper and it may come back in shreds!

But despite the need for a giant pooper-scooper and an inexhaustible supply of plastic gloves, if you have a Big Dog in your kennel you would be reluctant to get rid of him. Even when the mess and noise are unbearable, there is a part of you that is convinced that "she just might pull it off." She is impossible to discipline and is invariably late to meetings, if she shows up at all. She is always the center of attention and can hold a room with her easy manner, electrifying stories and pure charisma.

A skilled dog trainer can spot potential Big Dogs early on in the puppy stage. Sometimes it's in the glint of their eyes, the stagger of their walk, or a bark that carries a more confident tone than others.

As they mature, they become brash and bold and their learning curves can be difficult and costly. When fully grown, these Big Dogs become sales managers, corporate executives and entrepreneurs. In multilevel marketing, it's not uncommon for Big Dogs to be handed outright fully mature downlines (they would never build these from the ground level).

If they are groomed at an early stage, they can develop into top-producing SalesDogs, but dog trainers must always beware. Big Dogs are never satisfied with occupying the lower rungs on the ladder. They want to know the fast track on how to get to the top RIGHT NOW. They want you to—"Show Me the Money!"

They also have a keen sense of smell for picking out the power brokers and the right dogs to mix with. They don't like authority, and a small dog has a snowball's chance in hell of keeping Big Dog on the leash. They can't stand yipping. They'll insist on the corner office with a view, country club memberships and the platinum expense card. They want to be boss and want to know the quickest way to get there.

Although more prevalent in some breeds than others, Big Dogs come in all types. It only takes one Big Deal to create

BIG DOG!

a Big Dog, and once you graduate to Big Dog there is no going back.

Big Dog attacks can be nasty. To these guys all game is fair game, and God help the manager who tries to talk "territories." They pillage and plunder with reckless abandon, leaving terrorized prospects, frayed nerves and dumbstruck clients in their wake. They'll definitely bring home the bacon, but they'll clear out the hog house in the process.

Many Poodles are Big Dog wannabes from the moment they enter the kennel. They strive to earn the glory, the attention and the compensation that the Big Dog gets. They already have the image and the flash gear but their ultimate goal is to be able to actually afford to look that good!

Retrievers can be tremendously effective Big Dogs, but they might not be immediately obvious to you. That confidence and ability will still be there but it won't smack you in the face! Not only are Retriever Big Dogs able to close the big deals, but through their legendary commitment to service, they can maintain that deal for quite some time to come. The Big Deals are harder to come by for Retrievers, because they are not just concerned with the sale, but with what is right for the client. Most of their plans require considerable resources, patience and time to pay off. But when they do, their attention to the client relationship will have the Big Dog Retriever basking in the sun for a very long time.

Big Dogs are not big on implementation or follow-through, but when it comes to charming and building rapport they have the best that the Basset has to offer. They can stand toe-to-toe with any CEO and can win their hearts, their confidence and their financial commitment in a powerfully seductive and mysterious way that only the Big Dog knows.

There is one thing all of the Big Dogs share—they have very big hearts (although the Pit Bulls and Chihuahuas often have difficulty expressing it). Big Dogs love to take the local stray or young pup under their wing, protect the weak, nurture their friends and be seen as someone's "best buddy." In a time of need, or if your back is to the wall, the Big Dog will be there. A true hero, a Big Dog can love you to death and make a slobbering mess one minute and take on a pack of coyotes single-handed the next.

In truth, the everyday average breed may outsell the hybrid Big Dog most of the time, due to sheer effort and sheer volume. But when the big deal comes around, you'll need a Big Dog around to handle the close.

If you have Big Dogs working for you, sometimes you'll love them and sometimes you'll hate them. You have to treat them differently and when you do, you'll hear it from the rest of the dogs in the kennel.

Yes, Big Dogs can be a real pain in the behind. But when they land that big deal, and you crack open the champagne and cigars, it's easy to forget all of the times they drove you nuts!

The Right Pooch for the Right Prey!

(OR, DON'T SEND A HAIRLESS PEKINESE TO ICELAND!)

Early in my sales career, I took a position at UNISYS (then called Burroughs). At the time, UNISYS was a well-known computer and calculator manufacturer. As a new recruit and a fresh entry into the official world of sales in the Honolulu division, I worked under a branch manager who had been a highly successful sales representative. He was a Big Dog.

More than that, he was a Pit Bull Big Dog.

My manager was a world-class salesperson, having earned top commissions and respect in classic Pit Bull style. His formula for success was simple—to create a sales machine just like him. He attempted to jam everyone into his mold by forcing them to adopt the habits and strategies that worked for him. Massive barrages of cold calls, processed at lightning speed, slash-and-burn client relations and a total focus on new sales instead of nurturing old client relationships. "It's just a numbers game," he'd growl. "You either have it or you don't—just get out there and do it!"

And if he started losing faith in a sale, he wouldn't waste any time. There were only two words in the world that mattered—"yes" and "no." Anything else was a no and he would discard that prospect like a husk of corn and move onto the next prospect on the list.

But if it was a "yes," he would go for the jugular every time and shake them for everything that they had. His aggressive style was extremely effective for bringing in revenue, but he had little remorse for the devastation he left behind.

Having earned himself prestige as a top-flight Pit Bull, he was bound and determined to prove that his techniques would work at the management level. However, as successful as this strategy was for him as a SalesDog, he failed miserably in his attempt to be a Dog Trainer.

The problem was he thought that HIS WAY was the ONLY WAY. In reality, HIS WAY was just ONE WAY.

You can't change someone's basic, fundamental nature. It is their essence and their soul, and it makes each of us unique and special in our own way. You just can't make someone into something that is not part of who they are. Even if you shout, even if you scream, and even if you offer outrageous commissions!

So the result of this failed cloning process was a frustrated, unhappy and often crushed sales force, which led to huge staff turnover and dismal sales revenue by everyone but the few purebred Pit Bulls in the kennel—it was the classic 80/20 rule. After a few weeks, I was also scanning the ads for a new job and trying to figure out how to pay my rent.

It wasn't long before a new sales manager was brought in. His name was Steve—another Big Dog, but with entirely different skills. He was the antithesis of my first manager. He was a Retriever Big Dog—a rare and magnificent animal.

I remember our first sales meeting with him. He lumbered into the dimly lit conference room, which reminded me of some kind of cave. This cave housed about a dozen nervous and anxious sales reps, including myself.

We had just survived a hostile Big Dog Pit Bull in full frontal assault, so we were all pretty low on confidence and patience. Many of us already had one paw out the door. But we were mostly young scrawny pups, itchy and nervous, and although we were hungry and cranky we were still anxious to make our mark.

Although there was a lot of yipping and sniping going on, everything became silent as soon as Steve entered the room. Clearly, he was The Big Dog. Though new to the branch, he was eager to reveal his plan to turn this mediocre performing territory into something really special.

Did we care? Hardly. I learned a lot from those very early days. I definitely learned about my own brooding doglike tendencies as Steve proceeded to announce the changing of territories for the sales staff. If anyone doubts the correlation between dogs and salespeople, I ask you to recall the last time that you experienced territories being changed or commissions being altered, or the rules of the game being changed halfway through the game.

I can still clearly remember the sound of howling, whining and yelping at that meeting. The belligerent grumbling continued for days—often reaching fever pitch around the water cooler or during coffee breaks.

But the protests and whining never deterred our new manager. Steve was a large fellow with a big broad smile and a booming voice. He was kind of like a big old Saint Bernard of a man. He was strong and friendly, but he could turn sarcastic and nasty in a heartbeat.

He had a tendency to show up when you were just about out of food, without warmth and with not a friend left in the world. Then he would offer you a life-saving swig of energy to get you over the hump and through the storm. He could track you down anywhere (and he did!) and seemed to be able to carry any load. He was also a BIG believer in training, something my first manager rejected.

Yet what he did after that meeting was the most significant. He sat each of us down individually and got to know us, know our habits, our social lives, our personalities and our hobbies. I recall that he seemed to listen a lot more than he spoke. After each meeting he set out specific tasks for each of us, which were slightly different from person to person. Some reps went immediately to making "cold" calls, some interviewed only existing clients, others did market research on competitors and some tagged along with the service technicians.

He had the Pit Bulls making cold calls. He had the Retrievers making customer service visits. The Chihuahuas were conducting market research, while the Poodles were schmoozing key prospects. Meanwhile the Bassets worked on strengthening the relationships with some of the biggest clients.

He acknowledged the breeds of the kennel and put people in positions where they could succeed. But Steve didn't rest there. He took it one step further.

He worked on developing us, both individually and as a group, to be stronger and more efficient. We learned the talent of our own breed, while acquiring some of the skills of the other breeds.

The Chihuahuas learned how to make dynamic presentations, the Retrievers learned how to cold call and the Pit Bulls learned how to have patience and to listen. We were not squeezed into becoming something we were not—we were simply rewarded for being who we were while we were also encouraged to become more of who we were. It was an extension of ourselves rather than a denial of ourselves, and that made all the difference.

Each one of us was coached and trained according to our own personal strengths. Steve spent a great deal of time learning our strengths and developing them early. And Burroughs spent a ton of money sending us to training classes all over the country—but their commitment certainly paid off.

Once one of the worst-performing branches for Burroughs, our branch became an awesome selling machine. Within eighteen months, we became the number-one branch (per capita sales) in the country. (And I became number one in the U.S.)

Steve took the time to identify the breeds of dogs he had working for him and, as a good trainer, proceeded to groom us all to be fierce hunters, loyal companions and voracious learners. Each of us took something with us from that job that we carried through the rest of our lives.

Bone: One reason some dogs can sell and others cannot is not an innate selling gene or random luck, but that some are trained and some are not. True, there are some naturals, but very few. Great performers are coached and counseled to excellence. Strays, who get no training and never realize their own strengths or weaknesses, often end up mean and starving.

I learned a lot in those days about sales, people, behavior and the effect of attitudes on results. Over the years I have had extraordinary success in selling everything from cucumbers door-to-door, to calculators, computers, software systems, air freight and transportation services. I've sold services such as personal development, corporate change projects and behavioral change to the skeptical and uncommitted.

Little did I know at the time that my business life would school me into becoming a true trainer of "human type" and a veterinarian to those herds and flocks that required attitude adjustments. Now I travel throughout the world with my chair, whip and doggy treats as I work with thousands of other organizations that require assistance to turn their mutts into pedigree champions.

For all of the unnamed real-estate, insurance, network-marketing and corporate sales managers out there, I can say there is hope. For all of the masses of entrepreneurs, owners and salespeople seeking the "big financial enchilada," it's closer than you think.

Truly the best salespeople in the world, whether they be in Singapore, Hong Kong, Moline, Dayton or Manchester, have one thing in common. They are all SALESDOGS. And any person who is responsible for motivating, teaching or managing such a pack of dogs is a DOG TRAINER.

Strengths of the Breeds

On the secret of success, most great athletes will say, "Play to your strength!"

The Pit Bull, Retriever, Poodle, Chihuahua and Basset all play a vital role in the sales process. Unlike the canine world, "pure breeds" aren't usually as valuable as those with a bit of genetic mix. The key to being a Champion SalesDog is understanding and operating from your strength, while acquiring the positive traits of other breeds. This ability to "cross-train" in order to become the "best of breeds" is an essential ingredient of SalesDog success.

The first step toward this goal is to clearly understand the natural talents of the individual breeds.

Pit Bull

The Pit Bull's strength is clearly his or her **directness** and aggressiveness. There is no other breed more skilled at finding the shortest path between lead and close. What they lack in patience and often tact, they make up for in fearlessness.

It is their willingness to take on challenges head on that makes them successful in the market. Their relentless approach to taking on new prospects, making cold calls and handling objections is legendary, to the point of creating a stereotype that others attempt to emulate contrary to their natural tendencies.

While other breeds can be thrown off course with a "No," a negative response only makes the Pit Bulls work harder for the next "Yes." They don't waste time chasing after pipe dream accounts and are quick to move on if a lead proves to be slow in developing.

They turn objections into positives rather than researching, downplaying or avoiding them. A great SalesDog has the courage to take products and services into the marketplace

Bone from the Pit Bull: *When in doubt do something. . . . Do ANYTHING!* When feeling out of sorts, just make a sales call. Norman Schwarzkopf, the successful general of the Middle East Desert Storm campaign in 1991, said, "When in doubt, make a decision anyway. Making no decision can be catastrophic, while even a bad decision creates movement, action and can be corrected upon." This habit will open more doors and generate more momentum than you would ever imagine possible. When doubt strikes, deliberately override it with any form of action that puts you in front of someone. Sales is like baseball—the more times you swing the bat, the better chance you'll have of hitting a home run. You can't get anywhere sitting on the bench!

boldly and with conviction. Pit Bulls are courageous pioneers with a talent to develop virgin territories. When time is short and prospects are plentiful, these SalesDogs will have a great chance for success.

Some people in sales say, "It's a numbers game," and this is correct in some markets. If your product or service has a mass-market appeal then this mantra is definitely true and the Pit Bull is the perfect pooch for the job. But if you have a niche market where prospects are fewer, it is more likely that one of the other breeds is going to have greater success.

Golden Retriever

The Retriever knows that providing great ongoing **service** is one of the greatest wealth builders of all. He understands that quite often, the greatest opportunity for sales is within his own client base. When you provide quality and service to clients before, during and after the sale, future sales become easy.

The Retriever, like the Poodle, knows that happy users not only continue to buy, but they are a great source of powerful testimonials and quality referrals. Retrievers upsell and cross-sell while the other dogs are out looking for new prey. They know that it takes six times more money, time and effort to sell to a new client than it does to sell to an existing client.

Long term, Retrievers are the SalesDogs that can build strong sales organizations and lifelong, loyal customers. Despite their friendly nature, these SalesDogs are not naive. They have a clear understanding of what the long-term buying potential is of each client that they land and dish out their service accordingly. Retrievers don't have clients—they have friends, colleagues, associates who are all "wonderful people." (It's just that some of these people are more wonderful than others!)

One of their greatest traits is to constantly seek to add real value to each transaction and each service. They never tire of coming back again and again to find new ways to please.

Because of their commitment to providing a high level of service, Retrievers are not as comfortable with objections, because they often take them very personally. They tend to look at those objections as valid criticism of the product or service—or even worse, themselves. Customers love this, because they know that the Retriever will take the objection and bend over backward to make the correction and provide even better service and become even more accommodating.

Bone from the Retriever: *Always be the first to give!* This is true in a negotiation, a sale, an argument and in all different aspects of business. The person who gives first always has the advantage. By doing so, you tip the equality and fairness scale in your favor. The other party feels somewhat of a subconscious obligation to return the favor. By offering to others, you may get nothing in return immediately, but this energy business that we call sales and life has a funny way of reciprocating. Make it a habit, so that the gesture is sincere and not contrived.

Poodle

In business, appearance and image are important. Many inferior products and services can outsell superior ones, simply by appearing to be better. Perception is more powerful than reality!

No one knows better than the Poodle that image and reputation are important to sales success. Poodles are the consummate **marketing** SalesDogs. Their ability to position their products and services can make them among the highest-paid SalesDogs in the kennel.

They realize that the better they market their product or service, the easier it will be to reach their ultimate goal of becoming an "order taker." They want their consumers to come to them—not the other way around. Many Poodles are extremely skilled at developing and implementing marketing tools and strategies. They shine at seminars, trade shows and public-relations events. Poodles are excellent at building referral bases, using testimonials, and they can network with the best of them.

Bone from the poodle: *Learn to speak well to groups* and practice this art as often as you can. Having one-on-one skills is important, but being able to speak before a crowd will increase your exposure and confidence a hundredfold. Also *learn how to present yourself physically through grooming and attire.* Studies show that well-groomed and well-dressed salespeople sold as much as 35 percent more than those who did not take such pride in their appearance. Having been blessed by working with the best image consultants in the world throughout my career, I would recommend you seek professional coaching. Learn how to maximize your impact through dress and grooming. Learn how to accentuate your best features and minimize your others! People buy on image and impulse—looking good is just part of the job. A great SalesDog has a lot to learn from the Poodle.

Keep in mind that with Poodles, the product or service must not only be good—it must "look good, feel good and sound good" as well. They know that superior products and services can blow the competition away if they are able to combine aesthetics with great performance.

Poodles are great in companies where they have freedom to develop and test marketing tools. They love to build teams, networks and associates that they call "friends." They also shine where the product has a certain inherent flash and sex appeal, like cars, homes, resorts and expensive home electronics. Their strength is the effective portrayal of the corporate image.

Chihuahua

In this age of high-tech sales and marketing the Chihuahua is a rapidly emerging star in the kennel. Having current and accurate **product knowledge** can be a real challenge. But product knowledge is the proof, and without proof, you'll never fully convince the jury. The Chihuahua plays an absolutely critical role in closing the deal.

With customers becoming more and more savvy about the nature of the products and services in the market, a successful SalesDog must be current and precise. Too many lazy dogs don't place enough importance on this area, and because of this they suffer from the "superficial sell." Everything sounds great, until the client asks for specifics.

Chihuahuas are exceptionally gifted at putting together the facts and evidence that will show the prospects how everything works. They have the ability to alleviate fear and to impart wisdom and confidence in the product. Many of the best Chihuahuas have spent so much time researching and learning to understand the intricacies of the offering that they become genuinely passionate about the products or services they sell. Their unique combination of passion and irrefutable evidence makes them awesome sellers, capable of converting even the most skeptical of prospects. You just can't argue with the data!

Because of this quality, they also have a lower rate of buyer remorse than, say, the Pit Bull or the Poodle. Where a Pit Bull "victim" may have second thoughts once the intimidation has worn off, and the Poodle prey may think twice after the charmer has left, the Chihuahua's target is left with only facts, figures and statistics that equate to logic and credibility (especially for the left-brain folks!).

Bone from the Chihuahua: *Learn how to learn!* Get to know your specific learning strategy and learn how to absorb critical material like a sponge. You have a unique learning style that is independent of your breed. Once you know it, research and learning become fun and easy. When education becomes enjoyable, the sky's the limit. School taught you to listen, read, take notes and then regurgitate the information. Dogs don't do that, nor do most people. The order of learning for most of us is: experience first (make a sales call), talk about it afterward (discuss and review), then write down what you learned. The same is true with data. Visit a site, talk to a customer, interview a vendor, then explain what you learned to someone else, and then write down what you need to remember. Your retention rate will jump dramatically, and you'll be in great shape when meeting with prospects.

Chihuahuas are also naturally curious and are fascinated by their prospect's business and dreams. They are interested in everything and are therefore very good at matching product capabilities with client needs.

Their minds are constantly expanding data banks, eagerly performing twenty-four-hour-a-day market research on everything and anything. They possess more trivial information than would seem possible. But every once in a while it is that trivia, that smallest of details, that can shift the balance in your favor and clinch the sale. In the face of an objection, Chihuahuas are quick to get the facts behind the objection and match them to the real facts about the product or service. Their motto is: "He who possesses the most knowledge, wins!"

Basset Hound

The strengths of the Basset Hound are truly time-tested. Many members of this breed are from the Industrial Age—a time when values and personal relationships were the key ingredient to making sales. Their strength is just as critical in the Information Age, with so many relationships intertwined in each transaction.

Behind those big eyes and floppy ears is a huge heart of **INTEGRITY, CONSISTENCY** and **TRUSTWORTHINESS.** Basset Hounds carry these values to the marketplace as their badge of honor! They will go to great lengths to prove their dependability and loyalty. As a matter of fact, they can be very hurt when a client does not show them the same courtesy. When given all the options, they would prefer to be one-on-one with someone, looking him "square in the eye" and building personal rapport with him. They are very much like the Retriever in this way, in that they are very personable and lovable characters.

Bone from the Basset Hound: *Master the art of building rapport.* You can improve today by doing two things.

1. Learn to listen. Basset Hounds have big ears and do it naturally. Learn this skill by practicing listening with your eyes closed or with your head casually turned away from the speaker (ear directed toward the sound). If you are like most people, you are probably easily distracted visually. This will improve your ability to track a conversation exponentially. This technique is instinctive to great listeners.

2. Learn to match body language and modality language of the person you are talking to. The Basset Hound gets you to say "Awwwwww" because you identify with those big droopy eyes. You do the same with your prospect, wife, husband, partner or boss. Match their folded arms, crossed legs, tilt of the head, facial expressions, etc. Also match their language preferences. Are they talking in visual language ("Can you **see** what I mean?"), auditory language ("Do you **hear** what I'm saying?") or kinesthetic language ("It just doesn't **feel** right")? People will actually litter their speech with hints that will help you gauge their communication style. Listen for them and match these things in your speaking and you will create a magical connection without the other person even knowing it.

In an environment where achieving consumer loyalty can be a difficult challenge, the Basset Hound can have a big impact on customer retention. As the customer expectations and demands increase, the potential for competitive advantage and differentiation between brands diminishes, and it is the Basset Hound's ability to create emotional connection with people that is often the deciding factor for repeat business. Having a few Bassets in the kennel is paramount for ongoing sales success.

These SalesDogs can dig up and find leads where no one else can. If leads are sparse, you need a Basset to review the territory to sniff out the opportunities that lie beyond the obvious. These dogs are legendary for picking up scents when everyone else has long gone. They can sniff out potential at a thousand paces and have an uncanny knack of finding new and unusual solutions to client problems that no one else would have thought of in a million years.

Bassets instill trust in people around them. They are steady and dependable and clients will turn to them for impartial, unbiased advice knowing that they will get it. If the product or service isn't right for the client, the Basset, more than any other breed, is likely to tell the client. However, Bassets have a "mad inventor" quality that means that they are also more likely to find a hybrid solution that exactly matches the clients' needs *AND* gets them the sale.

Each breed must learn to balance its strength with some of the characteristics of the other SalesDogs. That is why a SalesDog TEAM is so valuable in today's marketplace. Each member can play to his or her talent as colleagues play to theirs. In this way, they can sell as a team with balance and effectiveness in a very natural way.

For example, Basset Hounds must learn to combine the richness of their deep values and ability to forge relationships with the marketing prowess of the Poodle. Otherwise they will not survive the burgeoning network and Internet economies—where you may never even SEE 90 percent of your customers! To keep pace with the others, the Basset must learn to prosper in more than just a one-on-one environment.

The Poodle and the Pit Bull can learn a great deal from the Retriever. While both of the former breeds are great at getting the sale, the Retriever understands the importance of the relationship after the sale for ongoing sales success.

All of the breeds have something to learn from the Chihuahua. Without these highly knowledgeable SalesDogs in the kennel, a sales organization would simply be all bark and no bite. The Chihuahua provides the critical facts and information that answer the client's most pressing concerns, allay their fears and ultimately get the ink on the paper.

So, what type of SalesDog are you?

Have you decided yet which breed you most identify with?

Which of the descriptions seems to ring the truest for you?

Which breed is your "significant other"?

As a Dog Trainer, your ability to identify your pack members greatly enhances your ability to manage the group. Knowing how to spot breeds will allow much greater penetration as you become better able to address more of the needs of more customers. The result? More sales, more commissions and more cash for everyone!

Note on Sales Support

Every sales organization also has an engine room. These are the people that turn the wheels on a daily basis and make sure that the products get from A to B, that the service is provided, that the client's name is spelled correctly. They bank the money and balance the books and try to keep everyone happy. These are the unsung heroes that are also critical for success. SalesDogs can reap large benefits by serving those that serve them.

The SuperMutt

At this point you may be thinking that you are a lot like one breed, but recognize traits of one of the other breeds too, and you may be confused. If you think you are more than one breed—you probably are. Each of us has a dominant breed with a little something else thrown in!

In the canine world, pure breeds are prized and expensive animals. In the world of the SalesDog they are just as expensive and uncommon, but perhaps not so prized! Some salespeople are proud members of a single breed and refuse to adopt the qualities of others. However, the most successful salespeople are those who understand their natural strengths and work hard to acquire the favorable traits of other breeds. In the world of SalesDogs, the SuperMutt rules.

I have a friend in Texas who is one of the most brilliant business owners that I know. She was formerly the top real-estate agent in Austin. Now she and her husband own the most successful real-estate school in the state. She is definitely a Pit Bull in Poodle clothing. She is tenacious and merciless in business, but can genuinely charm the socks off you with her grace, charm and beauty. As a matter of fact, the most potent and potentially lethal dog of any pack is the female mutt—specifically the Pit Bull in Poodle clothing. (And they are just as devastating at breaking your heart!)

Dogs like these amaze people with their ability to take large bites of market share without the competition knowing they've even been bitten. Moreover, prospects are so wooed and smitten by their grace and elegance that they are frequently unaware that they are being sold. You may have seen one of these cross-bred canines in the women's rest room reapplying her makeup in the mirror while muttering under her breath, "I am going to get that SOB!"

With the Poodle/Pit Bull Mutt, the "game" is the issue. Most purebred Pit Bulls couldn't care less about the commission once they latch on to the deal. All they care about is WINNING! But because Poodle/Pit Bull Mutts have a large strain of Poodle in them, the Pit Bull personality isn't allowed to rise to the surface. The prospects mostly experience that charm, wit and social ambiance that only the Poodle uses so well (Grandma, what big teeth you have!).

My father, who is one of the best salespeople I have ever met, is a Pit Bull in a Basset Hound uniform. You can see his beguiling, easygoing manner lulling prospects into their comfort zone. But if you watch closely, you can see the killer instinct flash in and out of his eyes. His aggression lies deep and goes unnoticed by the prospect. It's an odd thing to witness such a combination of begging and attacking.

Bones for the Manager

Never underestimate any SalesDog. One thing about dogs that can hunt is that they often appear to be lazy mongrels lounging around in an ineffective haze. That is, until they catch the scent, the adrenaline starts to pump, their hair stands on end and they're off. All hell breaks loose in a furious expense of energy as they put their nose to the ground and fearlessly track through mud, across rivers and over rocks until they ultimately land their prey.

Some SalesDogs talk a great story but are a little light on closing the deals. You have to know what you are good at and what skills you still need to work on. If you are a ten-pound Chihuahua and you come up against a five-hundred-pound brown bear, you may need a little backup to land the deal. Never be afraid to bring in another kennelmate with the necessary skills to close the sale. When done correctly, sales can be a wonderful team sport. Combine a Chihuahua with a Big Dog, for example, and you have the swagger and confidence with the facts and credibility to form a lethal combination.

There are also those SalesDogs who seem to be able to pick up a scent and follow it where no one else can. They have lots of qualified prospects but seem to have a hard time closing them. Let them play to their strengths and give them the support to finish the deals. There are others with dead noses. They cannot pick up or recognize a lead if they are hit over the head with one. But if you put them in front of a live prospect, they can charm, win and close them with ease and style.

Ultimate Bone

Play to your strength, let everyone play to theirs and you'll all be playing to win.

7

Play to Your Strength

I am a firm believer that you should know your strength and play to it. Yet sometimes your strengths can get in the way of excellence.

Early on in my career, I discovered this to be true for myself. One of my natural attributes is that I am skilled at studying, analyzing and adapting the qualities of others. I have spent a good deal of time admiring and researching the success of others. I have always figured that if they were more successful than me, there was something they had—some special trait that propelled them to the top. It became my goal to understand and acquire that trait.

Not bad thinking, except when it is taken to the extreme. When you totally mask your own spirit, spark and uniqueness to emulate someone else it becomes a deterrent to developing your own identity. You surrender your own strengths in the pursuit of acquiring the strengths of others.

The result for me was that there have been times when I

tried to actually become someone else. Don't get me wrong, modeling the strengths of others is one of the most powerful tactics you can use to increase your own power. However, I discovered very early on that trying to be someone else only ends in frustration, struggle, unhappiness and poor results.

Many of my friends, even to this day, are very strong, aggressive individuals. They have the ability to push and coerce others into agreement through sheer persistence, boldness, strength and power. While I enjoy participating in that energy, I have never been one to bully or confront others into a position of submission.

Growing up in the rural community of Navarre, Ohio, I was the littlest guy on the playground. I spent most of my recesses avoiding or escaping fights and skirmishes as a matter of survival. It was within this environment that I honed my natural ability to evade pursuers with quick starts, sudden changes in direction and running long distances at a moment's notice. When my legs failed me, it was my mouth that saved my lunch money. I learned how to talk my way out of difficult and threatening situations on a daily basis. As a result, I am sensitive to being too aggressive with people.

Many would think that with my lack of aggressiveness I would make a very poor salesperson. But fortunately, my personal success is proof to the contrary.

Truthfully, inside I am still very much that eight-year-old kid when it comes to confrontation and difficult situations. Whether it's a business dilemma, or disagreements with my wife or with colleagues, part of me still would rather run than fight.

If there is any appearance of courage, it is more due to my eternal naïveté about the harsh realities of the world than it is to any boldness in the face of conflict. I often find myself seemingly trapped in difficult situations, only to manage to wiggle out with seconds to spare. Through it all, I have found that my natural tendency to seek peace rather than war and my ability to turn nasty situations into favorable events have paid tremendous dividends.

My first job after graduating college was working with a successful airfreight trucking company. The company was led by an owner who decided I would make a good future president and leader of the organization. He was a dynamic entrepreneur who had overcome the odds to build a successful business. He wanted to "groom" me to take over one day.

I recall him saying on several occasions, "When you begin to think the way that I think, you'll be on the right track." This is the kind of thinking shared by many successful entrepreneurs.

Yet, I found that I did not have quite the stomach that he did for standing up to oversized truck drivers and for playing hardball with the unions. I learned that my strength was in my ability to negotiate and make others feel at ease. Eventually I grew tired of trying to force myself into a personality that did not fit me. I left that business to pursue a career in sales.

My first sales manager took the same approach, attempting to create us as carbon copies of himself—his version of the perfect salesperson. Once Steve replaced him, my whole world shifted.

The training I received during the first few months brought out my personal strengths: an unwavering desire to please clients, the ability to build instant rapport with people and an unshakable positive attitude. I could make friends with nearly anybody and quickly make them feel at ease. I found that once I encountered a quality prospect, I could build a very solid and trusting long-term relationship with him in a very short time (classic Basset/Retriever mix).

While my strengths were enough for me to develop into an above-average salesperson, I still lacked the balance of skills

I would need to be a truly exceptional SalesDog. Some of my natural tendencies actually undermined my success.

For example I was inclined to put off uncomfortable meetings and difficult tasks until "later." I often "kicked back" after a sale and relaxed, allowing the momentum and energy to die. This made it difficult to ever get on a "roll." So my natural tendencies ended up working both for and against me.

It was tough for me to make cold calls. I was not a Pit Bull in those days. Yet I realized that without this skill, I was always at risk when leads were slow. I knew I needed the ability to create business, and cold calls were the best way to accomplish this. It was clear that I needed to overcome the fear of talking to strangers as well as the fear of rejection that prevented me from making those calls.

My manager helped me get over this important wall by providing me with training. He explained to me that **the purpose of a cold call is not to sell anything,** but to train yourself for other sales situations. It is simply like lifting weights or running. He had me repeat the process over and over again in order to burn a neurological pathway in my brain. And it worked. The repetition eventually wore away the fear and created an excitement about taking on new challenges.

In fact, I turned the drudgery and my fear of making cold calls into a point of pride for myself. It became a game for me to see how many cold calls I could make in one day. I believe I still have the record: sixty-eight cold calls in one day!

In the past this would have never been possible. But I learned it could be a real blast. I remember running through office after office in downtown Honolulu, bursting through doorways, blowing past receptionists. I learned how to quickly spot and track down the office managers simply by their appearance and their location in the office.

I would descend upon them with an overpriced desktop

calculator under my arm in a wild demonstration that was equal parts lunacy, humor and shouting. That day, the first few calls were painful, but at some point during that record-setting day (somewhere around the twenty-fifth call) I lost it! I just came in howling like an attack dog with a case of hyena humor and put on a show for everyone in the office, never once thinking about making a sale or worrying about "looking good." My "skit" got better as the day progressed, as I continued to hone my skills with each new presentation.

As it turns out, no calls that day ended up in a sale, but the pathway in my brain was now permanently wired. I could run with the Pit Bulls if ever I needed to.

I realized that my SalesDog breed—a mix of Basset Hound and Golden Retriever—would someday need more skills in order for me to rise to the highest level. It took me only one day to appreciate the mindset of the Pit Bull and to acquire one of that breed's strongest traits—assertiveness and not caring what I looked like. It was a pivotal day for me and it has served me well ever since.

My newfound ability to confront difficult situations allowed me to build several lucrative businesses and has earned me a lot of money. Had I not been trained to embrace the best skills of other breeds of SalesDogs, while leveraging the strengths of my own, I might still be cowering in a corner someplace waiting for destiny to toss some scraps my way.

You do not have to be a Pit Bull, but you must learn what the Pit Bull knows and be able to use it when you need to.

I understand that **my greatest strength as a salesperson is that I am still a "nice guy."** But I can perform as a Pit Bull, Chihuahua or Poodle when necessary. With training and practice, the little voice in my brain became comfortable with new strategies and techniques. I was able to study, drill and extinguish any mental roadblocks that prevented me from taking on the success strategies of others. I have conditioned my brain to accept and activate whatever skills I need when a situation presents itself. The fears and barriers that held me back have just faded away.

Bone: Another reason some SalesDogs can sell and others cannot lies in the ability to learn and adopt winning skills. Those who are able to assimilate behavior and skills that are a bit foreign to them can learn to be the ultimate SalesDogs (or what we refer to as Super-Mutts). Those who cannot and refuse to budge from their stubborn mindset and belief patterns, saying, "It's just not me!" will always be the runts of the litter. You must always be a student, eager and willing to become more than you are.

The truth is that because I wanted to learn and because I was well-trained, I found that deep inside me there really was a Pit Bull that wanted to get loose. There really was a Poodle that wanted to prance and preen and "look good," and a chunk of Chihuahua that had tremendous passion and intensity and was a borderline data freak. There were diamonds deep within the coal mine. It took time and hard work to bring them to the surface, where they could be allowed to shine and make me wealthy.

However, if I had surrendered to the little voice in my head that responded to each challenge by saying, "I have to do it MY way," I would never have found the level of financial success, relationship success and joy of life that I enjoy today.

8

SuperMutt
Conditioning

So you may ask, "Which SalesDog is the most successful in sales and makes the most money?" Is it the Pit Bull for its tenacity? How about the Poodle for its ability to make a strong impression? Could it be the Basset Hound, because of its skill at making friends, or perhaps the Golden Retriever gets the nod for its unmatched customer service? Or in this electronic world, does the Chihuahua have the advantage with its head for technical knowledge?

The answer to the question varies from industry to industry and from situation to situation. You need a Poodle to be able to sell "the vision" of a new company. Often they are positioning what the company is "going to be" as opposed to "what it really is."

In a business-to-business, high-tech environment, the Chihuahua may be most successful at handling the tough questions and managing a complicated sale from lead to close. A Retriever might be most successful in damaged territories where rebuilding client confidence and loyalty can be best achieved through customer service–based strategies.

Then again it may be the role of the Basset Hound to come in and instill traditional values in a sales team in order to turn things around. The Bassets are the masters of selling to an "old boy" network. Of course, no one can drum up sales in slow or hard times like the Pit Bull.

So which breed is going to sell the most and make the most money? The correct answer is "All of them."

If you can find the best of breeds in one salesperson, then you have what we call the "SuperMutt." Regardless of the situation or environment, this champion SalesDog will be able to survive and thrive.

It is not what breed you are that will determine your success. SalesDogs that rely completely on the strength of their own breed, without acquiring important qualities of other breeds, will ultimately plateau in their sales. It's your ability to leverage your talent, while also acquiring the skills of the other breeds, that will make you an exceptional SalesDog. The more the mutt, the more the money!

SUPERMUTT

Not long ago, I was asked by the head of a large New York investment bank to observe a sales team that was struggling to increase their numbers. They wanted me to learn why and to turn their performance around.

So I started by sitting in on a conference call between the sales team and a client. We gathered in a glass-walled meeting room overlooking the bustling city. In the middle of the room was a large, polished mahogany conference table that could comfortably seat a dozen people. Pacing the room were six sales and marketing managers who were trying to sell a portfolio of high-profile investments to a Fortune 500 company's pension fund manager.

The three minutes before the call seemed to last an eternity. The suited gladiators in the room were hyped, like a high-school football team getting ready to head out to the field.

Their pupils were dilated, their palms were sweaty and their $250 ties were loosened for the attack. As the midday sun streamed through the glass-walled room I was momentarily blinded by the glint coming off several sets of gold cufflinks!

While I sat in the corner, quietly observing the scene, the sales team reviewed their game plan. They went over all of the possible objections that the client might bring up and the head of the bank pumped them up with a fiery, "We are going to NAIL this one!" I could almost imagine him wearing a whistle and a sweatshirt with the word "Coach" on it.

The phone rang and everyone's attention turned to the speakerphone in the middle of the table. After a few minutes of conversation and questioning, one of the SalesDogs lit up like a light bulb. He quickly reached over and hit the "mute" button on the phone.

Excitedly, he told the others that he had just come up with the perfect solution that was too good for the client to refuse. In a frenzy of agreement and shared enthusiasm they all descended on the plan. Like a pack of yipping coyotes, they jumped around, talked back and forth, scribbled feverishly on whiteboards and ran in and out of the room getting more data.

Oblivious to the ensuing commotion, the client was still rambling on, and not a single person was listening! The mute button was still on and every once in a while, one of the Sales-Dogs would turn it off and politely acknowledge the client, "Uh-huh, yeah, great, great." Then the mute button would be on again. It was almost surreal, and it was all I could do not to burst out laughing.

After a few moments, convinced they had their quarry cornered, the sales managers calmly sat back down and took off the mute. After pretending to listen for a few minutes, they found a pause and went for the jugular, delivering what they all thought to be the biggest win/win deal of the century. They hardly took a breath as the Chihuahua spewed forth data with the ferocity of a Pit Bull attack. At the end, they were all spent and I half expected them to light up cigarettes!

Then the client spoke. "Well, I hear what you are saying and I am not too sure. Why don't you give me a call in a few weeks and we can discuss it further. I need to look at a few more options."

As stunned disbelief descended on the conference room, a few feeble attempts were made to reignite the fuse but the customer simply signed off and hung up.

The sound of the phone clicking off was met with absolute silence—except for my snickering in the corner. The head of the bank, still numb and a bit confused, turned and asked me, "What went wrong?"

You didn't have to be a rocket scientist to figure out the problem. These guys were over-the-top Pit Bulls with a strain of Chihuahua. Clearly missing and sorely needed was any trace of Basset Hound or Retriever.

They were so busy creating solutions that they never bothered to hear what the problem was in the first place. The client tried in vain to voice his concerns about presenting the ideas to his board of directors. They failed to notice the importance of the story he shared with them in confidence.

He told how he embarrassed himself the last time one of these deals had gone sour on him. As a result, there was growing concern about the reputation of the bank as well as what the press was saying about companies that invested in these high-risk investment tools. Any Basset or Retriever worth its fur would have recognized that personal history was going to play a major role in the decision—this man was asking for trust, integrity, guarantees, peace of mind and then return. The pack of hounds only gave him returns.

Without sales team sensitivity to the issues, the deal didn't have a prayer. Worst of all, because they did not consummate the deal, they were now shifting blame on the client. Suddenly the client was "unsophisticated," "not our kind of client" and "high maintenance." To them it was the CUSTOMER'S issues—not theirs.

The good news is that we later trained those dogs in the best practices of the other breeds. I actually took these guys and had them sit knee-to-knee with each other. They were instructed to look each other in the eye without flinching while repeating simple commands that were given to them by their partner. I had them do this for hours. They hated it! Yet after a while, they *got* it. We burned a new neurological pathway in their brains. They learned an important skill of the Basset Hound, which is to engage, connect, listen and truly let the other person know that you understand.

From then on, this pack of SalesDogs went on to be the highest-producing sales division globally! Even while bond markets were crashing and all on Wall Street were running for cover, their sales kept going up. Each of these SalesDogs increased commissions by substantial six-digit figures over the next six months!

You must understand your strength and play to it. But through a specialized CONDITIONING process, you can implant the jewels of what any breed has to offer. This is the secret to becoming the ultimate SuperMutt SalesDog.

The conditioning and training process that I refer to is the repetition of drills and skills that may come naturally to other breeds, but are often foreign and repugnant to you. A German Shepherd may need to be walked on a short choker chain over and over until he learns to sit, stop and stay without flinching. In the same way, SalesDogs must be reconditioned through repetition in order to become great hunters and champions.

The primary purpose of the sixty-eight cold calls or the hours of knee-to-knee exercises or the presentation grilling in front of the room is *not* to make more calls or be good at eye contact or have snappy come-backs. It is to burn a path in your brain that instills the trait that you need to get rich now!

Let me explain this concept a little more, because it's important. The conditioning is designed to burn in a sensitivity that may not be there at all—as was the case with the investment banker Pit Bulls. They had no clue that they were missing something that the customer was desperately seeking.

I was once asked to provide feedback to a woman who was giving an important sales presentation to a group of investors. She had piercing blue eyes and gorgeous features and was dressed both tastefully and with a powerful flair. Her true sincerity and incredible knowledge of the investment opportunities she was going to explain matched her radiant smile and soothing voice.

The problem began when she started to talk. Not only was her presentation boring, but she was totally disconnected from the group. The audience "checked out," and people either nodded off or continually glanced at their watches. Her material was completely off the mark in terms of her target audience.

When I later asked her how she thought the presentation went, she said, "I thought it went great." I asked her why she felt that way and she responded by saying, "Well, they didn't ask any questions, so I figured it went well!"

I asked her, "If that is true, where have all the investors gone? I don't see any of them hanging around to sign up for more information or to write checks."

With a little more questioning, she slowly developed an awareness that she needed some help. It is almost impossible for most SalesDogs to coach themselves. They are on the stage so often that it is hard for them not to be blinded by the lights.

I can tell you that in over fifteen years of teaching others how to make powerful and effective presentations, this is unfortunately the most common scenario that I experience. Most SalesDogs have a lack of perception of what their audience, prospects and colleagues really think or how they are responding. This phenomenon is the "silent killer" of sales. These SalesDogs blame the environment, the market, the leads and clients—long before they take a good look at themselves in the mirror.

With training and coaching, SalesDogs get the opportunity to receive crucial feedback. In the case of my client, we proceeded to give her the presentation training that she needed. After only half a day of training, her seminar presentation statistics jumped through the roof.

Without training you just don't see what you don't see!

Another critical role of cross-breed conditioning is to counter the inborn fear of being rejected, embarrassed or humiliated. The reason people are afraid to make mistakes, face objections or try something new is that they are terrified of public humiliation (looking dumb in front of others). And for many, the fear of public humiliation is even greater than the fear of death. (Actually, death was number three on a list I read recently of major psychological fears!)

Dogs don't care because they were never laughed at in

school, never had their heart broken by a lover, and are rarely punished in front of large numbers of people and so forth. Therefore, the repetition of key drills in training is designed to heal the open subconscious wounds of the past. Replace those fears with automatic responses that generate excitement, joy and cash.

Big Bone

Many times we blindly believe that all our success is innate or natural. Sometimes we are even arrogant about it! "I gotta be me!" Every great company in the world researches and adopts the best practices of others in order to grow and remain competitive. A good SalesDog must do the same. Pride and ego must never be allowed to hinder the process of acquiring new skills.

Remember: You do not need to BE a Basset Hound, but you must learn what the Basset Hound knows and adopt his sensitivities to be a great SalesDog. Yes, it's important to know and understand your breed and all its strengths. But it's equally important to be aware of your breed's natural frailties and to be willing to improve upon them. Do not let your pride allow you to be "justified" or "right" about your approach. Do not ever say, "I have to ALWAYS do it MY WAY!"

That may have worked for Frank Sinatra, but this attitude leaves SalesDogs simply singing the blues.

9

Managing the Kennel

SALESDOG GROUND RULES

Obedience Training

Left on their own, without guidance or direction, even the most domesticated collection of dogs will quickly turn feral, snipping at one another and wandering aimlessly from territory to territory searching for a scrap of food.

SalesDogs are prone to the same behavior. If they are to achieve any kind of productivity, they need a trainer who can

NEVER UNDERESTIMATE THE TALENT OF YOUR DOGS!

identify the breed and understand the inherent strengths and weaknesses well enough to be able to put each pooch in the right position to succeed. They need a trainer who knows when to loosen the leash and let his SalesDogs run free, but who is also ready and willing to pull the choke-chain tight whenever one of his SalesDogs gets out of line.

In the world of SalesDogs, great salespeople come in different varieties and blends of the breeds. And it's important to understand that you do not have to be a purebred Pit Bull to be successful in sales.

One of the biggest myths this book is intended to dispel is the claim that there is only one mold for success in sales. If you are a frustrated Dog Trainer or a salesperson struggling to fit in with the rest of your pack, be encouraged. ALL DOGS CAN HUNT. You can be a "nice guy" with great integrity and with great compassion and heart and be a top SalesDog. You do *not* have to be a jerk, a sleaze, overly aggressive, a fan of cold calling or callous to win in this game.

You do not have to be a Pit Bull to be successful in sales. But you need to know what you are and what breeds are in your kennel so you can tailor your approach and your communication style.

Remember, just as SalesDogs have their unique personalities, so too do your clients and prospects. Matching your sales force with the proper clients, prospects and territories will help them in the beginning to learn how to build relationships. And as they progress and develop successful traits of several breeds, they will be able to succeed in almost any condition or territory.

For example, if you wanted to facilitate good rapport and maximize potential success, it would make sense to send a Retriever out after prospects that respond well to the Retriever style and send a Pit Bull when the prospect appreciates directness and speed. You wouldn't send a Poodle to a high-tech data freak—he would just look like a lightweight. Nor would you send a Basset to a Poodle prospect.

A Poodle or a Pit Bull may be eternally frustrated in selling government contracts, while the Basset or the Retriever may do well with the long and sometimes tedious to-ing and fro-ing that is required.

There are also certain products that lend themselves better to certain breeds. Pharmaceutical sales are somewhat void of traditional closing processes. It is strictly a relationship game where, over time, medical institutions purchase the drugs of their choice (Basset Hound territory). The Dog Trainer must help each Sales-Dog to be as successful as possible by helping to guide him in the appropriate direction. There is no single way to teach and develop your team. Training, and particularly coaching, must be tailored to each SalesDog according to the tendencies of the breed. But remember it's also very important not to overcategorize your hounds—each of them is different in his or her own unique way.

In managing Pit Bulls, it's important to issue them tons of challenges. They thrive on quotas, sales contests and ways in which they can pit their skills and results against others. Give them an impossible or high-risk challenge. "I know there is no way you're going to be able to hit this number. It's just impossible, but see what you can do." Give them the scent or an early win and let them run a bit wild.

This environment, on the other hand, would unsettle Retrievers because it puts them in a win/lose situation and Retrievers prefer to win/win. They dislike putting their own interests above anyone else's.

However, if you add a twist by introducing a supplementary contest that will measure customer satisfaction, you can use a Pit Bull technique to achieve a Retriever goal. Having a deep understanding of what motivates your SalesDogs will allow you to achieve the results you seek.

Your Pit Bulls aren't too concerned with your tact or even if you get a little gruff. They are happier in the locker room than the "golf club" and believe sales is a contact sport. Give them clear and CONCISE directions and send them on their way. You can send them cold-calling in dirty industrial parks and they won't complain. They are comfortable interviewing grizzled production supervisors, truck drivers or anyone who believes in rolling up his sleeves and putting in a hard day's work. If you need to generate activity in a sleeping territory, they are your breed. And always allow them time to tell you some of their "war stories" about how they met "insurmountable tasks" in the past, and let them go on the attack. They love it!

As long as they are active and chasing something they will be happy. They would rather be chasing their tail than sitting waiting patiently for things to happen. You should put that desire and energy to good use at all times.

Poodles must look good at all costs and that's the key to managing them successfully. Make sure that they know what it takes to obtain "top dog" status as a SalesDog. Allow them the leeway to make the "right" connections with the "right" people and they will do just fine. They probably love toys like palm-sized planners, Mont Blanc pens, jewelry, designer clothes and flash cars. Knowing that obsession is the secret to motivating a Poodle. You need to know what drives your people to success, and Poodles make this easy to understand because they wear it, drive it and just plain flaunt it for all the world to see!

Challenge Poodles by telling them that they have an opportunity to make a real "name" for themselves. Explain to them that if they play their cards right, they will have lots of people working for them and they may even become famous in the industry and community and may even someday write a book! They love the corner office with a great view and this alone can motivate them to perform near miracles for the corporate cause.

Motivate them by simply getting them to network with as many people as possible and get them to get referrals. Ask them to do presentations and be sure to invite important people to watch . . . they will stress out, but they will ultimately shine! Tell them that the more they present, the more they will become the force to be reckoned with and the easier their sales will become.

Allow your Retrievers to spend time with existing clients or prospects because they love to learn how to make people happy. Give them room on the leash to spend plenty of time with the client, learning and understanding how they can be of great service. Make sure they commit time to reporting back on how well your product or service helped the client, because this is the essential force driving your Retrievers. This breed is your best "back-end" seller. They will nose around like a detective looking for new and inventive ways to further help existing clients. This dedication to follow-up is what earns the Retriever a small fortune in additional sales, long after the initial commission has paid the mortgage.

If they feel they are "doing" something truly unique and important for your customers they will respond with heroic loyalty. You'll need to be very sensitive and responsive to product and service defects with your Retrievers, because they will judge your integrity based on how committed you are to their clients. Never back out of a warranty or promise you've made to your Retrievers' clients, or you will lose their trust and, consequently, sales will suffer.

On the other hand, if you respond to their service needs and promises, your Retrievers will march forward with seemingly cultist fervor for their products and services. There is no stopping a Retriever on a "mission to serve."

While a Pit Bull can walk away from a poorly executed sales pitch without an ounce of regret, your Retrievers can be affected very badly. Give them the support and training so that they are confident that they will be able to serve their prospects and clients with knowledge and professionalism and they will bring home the bacon every time.

With Chihuahuas, it's very important that you allow them time to immerse themselves in product analysis, industry data or local market research. For Chihuahuas, there is nothing more frightening than being asked a question they can't answer. For them, knowledge is power, and if you allow them to be "technically outdueled" by a prospect you might as well ship them off to the puppy madhouse.

As strange as it may seem to Dog Trainers of other breeds, Chihuahuas really DO need to know each and every detail about what they are selling. No other SalesDog has a better skill at turning seemingly obscure and useless information into deal-closing ammunition.

If they believe in the product or service, their tenacity and intensity make their arguments difficult to refute. Give them the accounts that love to compare features against the competition. They will have a field day and they will never give up.

The good thing is that the research the Chihuahua uncovers can benefit your whole kennel. Have them find all the ins and outs about the product or service, its advantages, quirks and benefits. Allow them to research the competition thoroughly so that they are clear on what makes their product or service truly unique and better. Once they have learned, they can give briefings to the rest of the pack at the kennel. This will get their juices flowing and give them a great sense of belonging and importance.

For Basset Hounds, tactfully remind them that their family is depending upon them to be an example and to be the breadwinner. It may seem like a cruel trick, but sometimes Bassets can be a little light on natural motivation and need a friendly nudge every once in a while.

You may have to push them out of the office periodically, as they can have a tendency to get a bit sedentary (aka lazy!). They like to curl up with a hot cup of coffee and "think" about things. Keep them out of the office and out of the local coffee shops and get them face-to-face with prospects where they can build the great relationships that they are capable of.

Bassets probably require the highest maintenance of all the breeds if you do not know their strengths. Give them a few good leads to sniff and let them know that a deal is just around the corner if they just stay with it. Praise them for their tracking ability and let them know that you will be there to support them at the close.

They are like the legendary television private investigator Columbo. Columbo was always seen as a nuisance and a bit of a lightweight because of his disheveled appearance. He would lull the suspect into a false sense of security and then—pounce! Bassets are exactly like this. Tell them that you need someone with a good sense of "deal" smell to dig up more leads and ferret out the buyers. Get them to find out who is buying what from whom.

Another particularly strong trait of Bassets is their ability to calm upset customers, especially in the case of a service failure or problem. Their one-to-one abilities and deep sense of integrity are incredible.

A Basset that I knew in the airfreight business was a true legend. His company was working with a $15 million pharmaceutical distribution account. This time-sensitive merchandise had to be delivered at very specific times to sometimes very obscure locations across the country. In the face of a series of horrendous service failures in which nearly half of the products arrived late, damaged or improperly documented, this Basset went in to the client, who was not only ready to shift the entire business to another carrier, but was withholding payment for damages. As a result of the this Basset's conversations with the client, however, not only did he save the account, he sold an additional $7.5 million of business to that same customer. That requires the sincerity, honesty and humbleness of the Basset.

Some Bassets, however, have a tendency to suffer from "Poodle Envy." It's important to make sure they understand that their innate abilities to make lots of good friends and build trust can allow them to compete with any of the breeds. A pat here and a dog biscuit there will go a long way.

Give them some extra room to spend quality time with their prospects. Through their unique abilities, they will be able to win deals that are virtually "unwinnable" with any of the other breeds.

The key in all SalesDog training is to remember that what works for one breed often does not work for others. Different things motivate different SalesDogs, and exceptional SalesDog trainers know that and tailor their approach to nurture each breed.

Pit Bulls and Poodles love to be champions and will do anything to achieve that, while for a friendly Basset Hound or a Chihuahua that may be secondary. The Golden Retriever just wants to know that someone loves him!

Know the breeds in your kennel!

Dianne, a million-dollar corporate sales winner, says it well:

A lot of sales is based on relationship, and service is a critical component for credibility through the initial sale process (you are being judged) and most importantly for ongoing customer loyalty. Service is where you continue to find out your customer's requirements—here is your opportunity for repeat business, to upsell and to cross-sell. Service is sales! You may have certain sales "dogs" that excel at the initial sale but not at service. Hence you and your organization must know what type of "dog" you are and if necessary bring in the rest of the pack to take care of ongoing service. The problem, on the other hand, is that if you focus only on quality customer service alone that will not bring in sales—you must continue to close, close, close the sale.

Dianne is a Pit Bull in Retriever clothing!

House-Training

The temperament and manner of any breed of dog is mostly determined by how they are raised. I have seen Rottweilers who were the gentlest creatures on earth and hand-sized Terriers that would take your arm off! To have a kennel full of well-trained and disciplined SalesDogs you must house-train them all and treat them with care and respect. Otherwise you will spend an inordinate amount of time with a pooper-scooper, plastic glove or muzzle cleaning up behind them and saving the neighbors' children!

All dogs need to be stroked and praised in order to grow up with a pleasant disposition. SalesDogs need that positive stroking too. Salespeople are simple animals. Just as the Golden Retriever wants to be scratched behind the ears, SalesDogs live for praise and ego stroking. Some SalesDogs have even been known to sacrifice financial reward for a glimpse of fame and praise. They live to be Legends.

I have never been an advocate of rubbing a dog's nose in its mess to get him to learn, although there are managers out there who take that approach with their SalesDogs. Typically those managers aren't getting nearly the sales results they could be getting with a more positive approach. To house-train any dog all you need to do is bury him with praise when he makes his mess outside. And correct him immediately and quickly when he doesn't.

SalesDogs are the same. When they finally do what you want them to do, shower them with acknowledgment. And be specific about what it is they have done right. "You did a great job last week" is too vague and lacks credibility. Also, be immediate with both praise and correction. "You did a great job today when you countered the client's objection on price—you must have really been listening to pick that up—well done." It reinforces the skill being acknowledged and makes them feel important because you paid attention to them.

Most breeds respond well to acknowledgment, while dogs that are constantly beaten and scolded either become junkyard mean or quivering wrecks. Neither is good for sales. Ignoring their behavior is the worst thing to do as it turns them into lazy, unruly mongrels.

One of my clients operates more than two hundred retail franchises. In a one-year period we found that sales per person were increased several percentage points simply by having store managers actively celebrate or acknowledge the wins of each of the store people. It does not take a lot of effort to activate Sales-Dogs' natural desire to win. Simply tell them "good dog!" and rub behind their ears occasionally or scratch their tummy!

To build a shared ethic and understanding among the kennel there must be a Code of Honor, Code of Conduct or "house rules" that all the dogs agree to live by.

TEN BASIC HOUSE RULES

1. **Don't pee or poop in the house.** If you make a mess, you are responsible for cleaning it up, regardless of the circumstances. Never dump your problems on others or where they do not belong.

2. **No needless or incessant barking, whining, sulking or yelping.** No finger-pointing, personal insults or complaining. Take responsibility. If you have a problem, address it directly to the person involved and do not go behind his or her back.

3. **Come when called.** Be accountable for your results.

4. **Don't chew or scratch the furniture.** Do not bad-mouth others on the team—ever. Especially in the company of prospects or clients.

5. **Stay off the furniture.** Never take undue advantage of another's support or position, whether they are kennelmates, prospects or customers.

6. **Don't beg at the dinner table.** Don't seek sympathy for poor results, lay blame or expect handouts. Earn your own meal ticket.

7. **Don't steal food off the table or counters or out of the refrigerator.** (My brother's dog can actually open the fridge herself and grab a snack!) Be honest and operate with integrity in all matters. Full disclosure in all cases.

8. **Don't wander off.** Respect each person's territory and always inform each other of possible conflict or overlap. Stay focused on the tasks at hand. No conflict of interest.

9. **Don't jump up on people.** Be clear on a common definition of being professional and all agree to always meet and maintain that image.

10. **Celebrate all wins.** Celebrate even small victories, both yours and others'.

These are just a few of the rules that will bind your pack, turning it from a disparate collection of dogs into a Championship SalesDog team. When the pressure is high and most dogs are running for cover, your SalesDogs will pull together and win.

Puppy Training

Getting your new pups up and running quickly is an art. Sales-Dogs that are not handled properly when they are young will be a problem forever. It's sweet and cute when a puppy jumps up on you—all that youthful exuberance. But when you are lying face up with 120 pounds of slobbering mutt sitting on your chest, it's suddenly not so cute, not to mention painful!

Unfortunately, I have met a few salespeople like this. It is easier to instill proper behavior when a SalesDog is new in his or her career than it is to correct him or her later on. Yes, Old Dogs can learn new tricks, but old habits die hard.

EINSTEIN

PUPPY PROBLEMS

Most pups do not master obedience training or become house-broken overnight, but with the right training you can get them to behave like Champs.

The process is fairly simple:

Start by giving your salespuppies small, easy tasks that will allow them to achieve early wins. Do not send them out selling in the beginning. Instead, assign them to read six product-related articles and report back to the group on what they have learned. Tell them to read three manuals and to give three demonstrations.

Have them visit ten installations and then have them share with the sales group what they learned. Have them go observe or work for your best customer at no charge for a few days.

Have them learn about the industry in which they will be working. If you sell real estate, spend some time with a builder, with a general contractor and with a lender. If you are selling insurance, go to the library and research the history of insurance business over the last five years. Scan all of the insurance-related headlines on the front page of *The Wall Street Journal* for the past year.

Years ago, one of the biggest prospects I had was in the food wholesale business. Because I knew nothing about the food wholesale business, I decided to study it firsthand. By sweeping floors and unloading trucks for a week at the warehouse, I learned more about their business than I could have ever gleaned from industry magazines or company profiles. Later they honored me with the biggest sale in the region that year.

Have them just make phone calls. Ask them to conduct phone surveys to find out what their customers want. Have them do at least twenty-five before they move forward.

Throw them some bones. Make sure each successfully completed task is acknowledged and celebrated with a high-five or a SalesDog pat on the head. It builds momentum and keeps them trotting on the path toward success.

Give your puppies a little time to grow up. Most managers throw the pups into the wild fully expecting some to die and some to survive. This is a waste of time and money and takes an unnecessary toll on the human spirit. Most dogs can hunt, but it takes a patient trainer. Remember, give them small, low-risk tasks!

Then when your SalesPups start graduating into making real live sales calls, they will not take setbacks too personally.

©EINSTEIN

PUPPY LOVE NEEDS TO BE MANAGED

They will have built up a head of steam that will carry them through the storms. Momentum is absolutely key to success for your sales team. Coach them, praise them and hold them accountable all the way through.

You can always tell when a puppy has grown up in a good home. How will your SalesDogs do when they are ready to go out into the real world? Teach them early with patience and respect and the payoff will be massive—for you and your pups.

Building a High-Performance SalesDog Team

So you've recognized your breeds, you've got your old dogs, you're breaking in your pups and you know who's who in the kennel. What now?

Ideally you want your pack of dogs to play and learn together in a spirit of fun and camaraderie, tempered with some appropriate discipline. Many managers are frustrated because their SalesDogs do not perform up to their level of expectation. This is usually because bad habits were established when they were pups or the expectations of the manager have not been articulated clearly enough.

Many managers make the mistake of ignoring the potential of building a great sales team—put off by the hard work and patience required. Some choose to leave SalesDog packs to their own devices, in which case it is the survival of the fittest, not necessarily the best. Because this atmosphere is damaging to certain breeds, the result is an unbalanced kennel where trust and teamwork fall prey to greed and backstabbing.

I have seen some managers use a divide-and-conquer approach that puts all the salespeople in direct competition with one another. Competition is good, but not when it is destructive. Because while this may build lots of initial activity and even push sales up in the short term, it creates high drama and a sometimes unruly atmosphere. Ultimately it will damage image, efficiency and results. Sales teams I have observed that follow that model behave like a pack of starving wild dogs, stealing each other's scraps, quarreling over the tiniest issues and preying mercilessly on the weakest in the pack. They tend to surround and consume small animals (deals) and quarrel over the remains rather than band together to take down the buffalo that they can all live off for weeks.

In contrast, examine the team of dogs that pulls a championship Iditarod sled team. This type of sales team can weather all odds and conquer untold adversity and will protect each other from the cold and elements. For the last twelve years we have helped organizations to build Championship Teams in which each member becomes a superstar in his or her own right and the results of the team are far greater than the sum of its parts.

A few years ago, one of my clients had received some very damaging press regarding questionable ethics and practices. I had been working with one sales team for about a year. They had developed a very tight Code of Honor and had learned, through much confrontation, that they could really trust each other. While the negative press had many high flyers bailing out of the company and running for cover, this group banded together to blow the roof off sales for their country and region. They viewed the press attack as a call to arms instead of a call to run for cover.

As the sled team sticks together and becomes fiercely loyal in adverse conditions, a well-coached team of SalesDogs will stand by their Code and never abandon teammates in need. The greatest sales efforts of all have always been by great teams.

Even though the manager may be the undisputed leader, you should never rule with an iron hand exclusively unless you are willing to show the soft and supportive side as well. No great coach ever gets away with being a tyrant forever. If your style is to be tough, you have to learn also how to show the soft side in order to let your dogs know that you are truly on their side. Each member of the sales team must be empowered to call questionable behavior as he sees it, as well as give lavish praise when due. As a matter of fact, the best sales managers that I have seen are those who leave the leashes loose enough so that the dogs can run, but short enough to keep them out of the traffic.

THE COMPANY SALES TEAM AT WORK

If you want to motivate any kennel or pack of dogs, there is a list that I enclose here that works for all teams. In our live training sessions and in the tape series, these items are developed in great depth and detail.

THE CHECKLIST FOR MOTIVATING HIGH-PERFORMANCE SALESDOG TEAMS (I CALL IT "THE LIST")

1. Celebrate all wins! Actively acknowledge all participation and tasks well done.
2. Establish the Code of Honor (house rules) and "call" breaches cleanly.
3. Debrief all wins and "learning experiences" early and often.
4. Use peer pressure to motivate the pack.
5. Don't try to teach pigs to sing! (more later).
6. Use common terms, such as "learning experiences" and "debriefing," rather than convoluted corporate-speak.
7. Feed the "hot hand." When one of your dogs is on a roll, keep fueling the fire until it cycles out.
8. Set short-duration goals that can be accomplished quickly and cleanly. Most dogs have very little concept of the future. They can scarcely think beyond dinnertime.
9. Get your dogs to practice standing in the "heat" of pressure, confrontation and challenge often so they will become used to it. Be sure to surface and acknowledge the emotion that arises. The SalesDog objection/rejection system systematically conditions the SalesDog to successfully deal with emotion.
10. Manage and address emotional needs more than tangible ones.

11. Give them a way to feel that they are contributing something to a higher purpose. Dogs love to serve.

12. Establish and maintain ritual behavior, events and routines that promote team, family and camaraderie.

13. Always look for champions and allies within the team and use them to lead the team.

14. Look for and acknowledge heroes all the time.

15. Find a way to change the environment, mood, routine or physical location when the team gets stuck mentally or emotionally. Dogs that lie on the couch too much get lethargic.

16. Manage and focus on energy and emotions continually.

17. Throw their problems back to them to solve. Toss the meat back to the wolves.

18. Practice the Roulette Wheel of Leadership. Whoever has the "hot" hand or the "hot" idea at the time is the spiritual leader of the group at that moment.

19. You can show your hard side when it comes to maintaining the rules of the game or the Code of Honor, but always balance it with the soft side (supportive).

20. Know when to facilitate others, when to be a champion and when to take momentary control.

21. When you sense something brewing, or a mindset sitting under the surface, bring it up and tell it like it is . . . as you see or sense it. (Even though you could be wrong!)

22. Be a student of people, psychology, management and change and DOGS!

Dogged Belief

FOUR MINDSETS OF
CHAMPION SALESDOGS

Humans seem to think that they have a complex brain. We have cortexes, limbic systems, reptilian brains and all sorts of other stuff! A big brain is handy for doing your taxes, remembering your anniversary or reading this book. But in sales, sometimes too much gray matter can get in the way.

Dogs, on the other hand, are very simple creatures with rather small brains. They usually react positively to whatever goes on around them because they do not overanalyze, over-theorize or overcriticize themselves. They live for the moment. They respond directly to simplicities of pain, pleasure, love and respect.

The Golden Retriever chasing after a Frisbee is entirely focused on success. He probably doesn't worry about all the times he's dropped the disk in the past. He probably doesn't lie awake at night panicking about whether he is going to be able to catch the Frisbee tomorrow. He just knows he wants to catch it now and nothing else matters!

If that were a human, by the time he got to the park he would be stressed to the max and worrying about what others would say if he dropped it. He'd wonder who he would be letting down if he dropped it and would be already thinking of excuses! The human brain has an amazing gift for linking totally unrelated events in order to come up with weird and wonderful belief systems, superstitions and rituals.

We sometimes come to complex conclusions whenever something out of the ordinary occurs—either good or bad. For example, you make a sales call and it goes particularly badly, you make a total mess of the presentation and the prospect is really rude.

Because our brain is ultimately a pleasure-seeking/pain-avoiding mechanism, it will search the environment for something unique that it can attribute these events to. The conclusion could be as ridiculous as "I washed my hair with new shampoo today." And if you have another painful experience (of any kind) *and* you used that same shampoo in the morning, you suddenly have a belief system that links pain to that shampoo—you will probably suddenly "go off" that shampoo. This is a very simplistic description, but the point is that we often tend to find correlations between totally unrelated items or events. It could take the form of an "unlucky" suit, the way you started your day or the last conversation with your boss.

The quality of your decisions determines the quality of the result. If your decisions are based on a faulty belief system then the results will be warped.

So remember, the next time you get knocked back, or asked to perform a difficult task, or you have to face a fear—see it for what it is in that moment. Just catch the Frisbee—be a dog!

Have you ever noticed that there are some people who seem to have the "magic touch"? It seems that no matter what they attempt, they achieve success. In more than twenty years of personal development, I have always wondered how that happens. I now believe that it is because they instinctively think like dogs.

Dogs have four basic mindset disciplines that, once integrated, can dramatically change the results in all areas of life. With these disciplines, you too can have that "magic touch."

Are you interested?

The first and critical question is "Are you willing to truly think like a dog?" If your ego can handle it, I am sure that your bank account will appreciate it, because these mindsets are the reasons some dogs can hunt—sell—and others never will.

These mindsets are all about how you mentally deal with four critical areas everyone encounters every day:

1. Taking on challenges or adversity: Face the challenge.
2. Responding to a negative experience: Trap negative dialogue.
3. Responding to a successful endeavor: Celebrate all wins.
4. Viewing yourself and others on your team: Project the power of your personal intention.

The success formula for all four points above takes only minutes to learn and seconds to apply and is guaranteed to positively affect all areas of your life. Enjoy more sales, more money, better health, peace of mind and happiness. This is a proven formula, one I've been using for more than fifteen years to help organizations make millions of dollars by coaching million-dollar SalesDogs, building Championship SalesDog sled teams, high-performance players and inspirational leaders.

Using these mindsets on a systematic basis has proven to improve sales by 30 percent to 80 percent. And it's even possible to test some of these mindsets in advance to predict and affect future performance.

1. Face the Challenge

Taking on a challenge or facing adversity can be intimidating and is often loaded with anxiety. Most high-performance dogs are able to take on very challenging tasks because of their conditioning and training. For inspiration, they rely on very simple memory banks that tell them that reward follows successful completion of their task. They don't remember the times they failed, unless these moments were linked to punishment or pain.

The Golden Retriever probably doesn't poison her mind with visions of failure. You can tell by her eager expression of pure excitement and enthusiasm that she fully anticipates success—she's going to get that stick. All she can see is the stroke, treat or cuddle that lies ahead. She relies on the successes of the past, while allowing the failures to slip on by. From her past, there are a series of memories of success that can be leveraged to give strength in the present and courage in the future.

When basketball legend Michael Jordan talks about how he handles the pressure of always having the ball in his hands at the end of any close game, he says, "I do not try to visualize it or hype myself into it."

Instead, he recalls in vivid detail the drama-filled closing seconds of the 1982 NCAA National Championship Finals when he made a twenty-two-footer from near the baseline to win the championship for North Carolina. He says that when a challenge is imminent, he pictures that moment in 1982, says to himself, "Okay, I have been here before," calms down and waits for something positive to emerge (from *Sacred Hoops*, by Phil Jackson).

Even when you haven't succeeded in exactly this situation, search for a similar experience from your past so that you can draw confidence and assurance from that event to assist you in the present moment.

SUMMARY

The present can create high emotion, which can yield low intelligence and as a result sometimes low resourcefulness. Strength can come from the past. You must learn to capture those successes and use them in the present.

2. Trap Negative Dialogue

The most phenomenal discipline you can implement is learning **how to trap the mental dialogue that occurs during adversity.**

Have you ever seen a dog get depressed about missing the Frisbee in front of the other dogs? Have you ever seen a dog give up after one try? Have you ever seen a dog skulk off and sit in the corner and tell himself how stupid he is for dropping the tennis ball? For that matter, have you ever seen a dog catch a cat? They have been chasing them for thousands of years and I doubt if any dog has ever caught the cat. Do they lie on the floor, with paws over their head, crying about how their life doesn't work? Or do they just find another cat!

Adversity is part of life. Getting knocked back is part of the natural testing and feedback process

DOG-ESTEEM IN BAD SHAPE

of life. You may burn your tongue on the soup a couple of times until you discover it is the right temperature to eat. It's testing!

You don't give up eating soup or eat only cold soup for the rest of your life.

Dogs keep their energy high and keep bouncing back until they get the response that they want. They don't need a formula, because it's in their blood.

SalesDogs, on the other hand, need the formula for winning in order to keep their brain from going into meltdown. Here are some keys to keeping your brain in check and concentrating on sales success.

First, contrary to many traditional New Age personal development programs, it is critical to know how to *externalize* the event. That means it is important to attribute the cause of the problem to circumstances *outside* your total control. In other words, shift the blame AWAY from you.

For example:

- Prospect having a bad day
- Bad timing
- Bad hair day
- Information that was unavailable to you
- Someone else's personal issues

Basically, it's important that you keep your mental house clean of any damaging trash. You can't allow a negative moment to be a reflection of any other part of your life, your business or your sales cycle. That one prospect rejected your cold call doesn't mean that your whole week is going to be bad. It doesn't mean that your sales cycle is inherently flawed or that you're not cut out to be a salesperson. And it doesn't mean that you'll never get your finances in order. That is all crazy big-brain thinking. A dog would never dream of making such wild and random correlations.

Being responsible does NOT mean that everything bad that happens to you is caused by you!

Making the assumption that you yourself are the sole cause of all negative experiences can be incredibly damaging to you. This doesn't mean that you don't learn from your mistakes. It just means that you don't allow your mistakes to ruin your mental well being. This ability to deal with and explain adversity can be found in the mindset of every great salesperson, sports player, team, coach and investor.

You *are* responsible for how you respond, what your next action will be or how you interpret the experience . . . but not necessarily the *cause of the experience itself.*

It does not even matter if your conclusion or interpretation is true! Your mind does not know the difference. If you interpret the cause to be you, your energy goes down. If you externalize it, your energy goes up. Remember that sales is a pure energy business, so as long as you keep the energy high, you will recover faster and sell more.

Second, tell yourself that the rejection is a specific occurrence and do not let your brain interpret it as having any long-lasting or extended significance. Take it for what it is—that a particular person does not have a particular need for your particular product or service at this particular time.

Here is the formula for dealing with a negative situation.

MEMORIZE THIS!

1. First, a problem occurs. It must be actually happening, like leaving your suit coat at the airport and realizing that you've forgotten it only after the plane has taken off! Or perhaps a prospect tells you that he no longer has a need for your product.

2. As soon as you discover the problem, you'll experience a flash of some sort of emotion. This must act as your alarm bell, telling you to be aware of what comes next.

3. The dialogue in your brain begins.

4. Within seconds of the dialogue starting, you must override it by asking yourself, *"What am I saying to myself right now?"* This question forces your brain to answer and you then step outside yourself and observe the internal dialogue.

5. You must first identify the REAL emotion—anger, frustration, disappointment and so forth. Ask, "**What is it that I am feeling right now?**" Once you have identified the emotion, say the word out loud. *"Ah ha—it's frustration!"* You can shout this out or whisper it depending on where you are and how you feel! Have fun with it . . . for example, say it in an Inspector Clouseau accent!

6. Within about ten seconds you can usually recognize that you are using a "universal" descriptive word, such as "always," "never," "every time," "all," or "every." For example: "This *always* happens to me" or "I'm *never* going to get this."

7. Upon recognizing the universal word, you should pause, put it in check, smile and say *"There it is!"* Spotting the word(s) is 95 percent of the battle toward instant recovery. The smile lightens the load and raises your energy level.

8. You must then mentally correct the universal words with something specific like "this time," "it just so happens that," "it turns out that," or "in this case it didn't work."

9. You should then spot the internal directive. "I," "me," "my fault," "what is it about me," "why me" and so forth.

10. Smile again and say *"There it is!"* Then find some way to lay blame, justify it or blow it off to logical circum-

stances. This part can be fun and humorous to do! "That guy was in a bad mood today." "With a toupee like that it's no wonder he's having a bad day!" "The competition was lucky this time—hey, there's room for all of us!"

11. Then, based upon whatever you told yourself, quickly create a stack of facts and evidence to justify what you told yourself. "I was tired from twenty-four hours of traveling and a bit burned out when I set down my jacket somewhere in that airport," or, "That guy was nice every other time I talked to him, it was just today that he was a jerk."

12. **Most important step:** Ask yourself this question: "How do I REALLY want to *feel* right now?" (optimistic, happy, excited, strong, confident and so forth). Ask the question to yourself and then try to actually get that feeling inside. If you cannot, think of an experience, vision or episode that will bring a small smile to your face. Once you do that, then hold the feeling for as long as you can (seconds, minutes, hours!?). This will shift the energy all around you. This is the magic part. Do not ask me why it works, just DO IT! I have found that once my emotions or feelings begin to change, everything else does too. **Example:** I say to myself, *"I would really rather feel happy right now."* I picture a scene of Benjamin scoring his first goal at soccer camp and his two little fists raised into the air as he explodes with joy. A smile is on my face. I hold it for a few seconds, anticipating my next present-time action, and the process is complete.

13. After all of this you should tell yourself to expect a good thing to happen soon. And then it does! The phone rings and someone from LAX security will tell

you they found your jacket, or you will get a call from a long-lost prospect who wants to see you.

This whole process takes about one minute maximum!

To sum up, if something negative happens, you have

to know how to tune in to your internal dialogue, how to trap the "little voice" in your head and steer it toward award-winning conversation. This technique is CRITICAL for generating sales at any level of business. It is critical to have a winning attitude about life! Have fun with adversity.

GETTING IN TOUCH

3. Celebrate All Wins

Responding to success when the wins start happening, or when anything positive happens, is an important two-step process. First, you have to get to CELEBRATE THE WIN! A physical "anchoring" of the win with a high-five, handshake, clenched fist or verbal "YEESSSSSS!" are all methods that most of us are familiar with. As a SalesDog, I suggest you at least give yourself a pat on the head or release a big howl at the moon.

These methods drive the moment deep into your mind, your spirit and your body for permanent strength. The cementing of that moment builds momentum for the next task. Over the years I have seen the most phenomenal shifts in people, organizations and performance as a result of continual acknowledgment and celebration of wins.

If you have ever watched sports on TV or even played yourself, you will know and accept that celebration is part of the game. Every time a player scores a point, gains a few yards, does something well, gets a hit or makes a catch, instinctively the rest of the players give him a high-five, a pat on the back, a head butt (not recommended) or something to acknowledge his contribution. There is no way a player in the NBA can score a basket without getting a high-five. That is why they are so achievement-oriented. Of all the techniques, this is probably the most powerful, yet least used by adults, because adults get embarrassed and think it's childish or unprofessional.

Several years ago, I worked with an overseas hotel. It was a good company with several hundred people on staff. Working with the heads of the departments, I coached them into the habit of always celebrating wins—not only their wins, but also the wins of their staff. This was not easy because the culture of many Asian regions does NOT include this kind of celebration. Yet over the months, the new habits began to sink in.

This hotel slowly but surely began to see the results as the entire staff overcame their reserved natural habits. The organization became a money-making sales machine. Their combined en-

CELEBRATE ALL WINS!

ergy was so high that during the last Asian economic downturn, when most other hotels in the region were operating at 40 to 50 percent occupancy, this hotel was 90 percent plus. They banded together and decided that *everyone* in the hotel was responsible for sales. In fact, the largest account was actually landed by members of the housekeeping department! The successful turn-around was a direct result of the constant acknowledgment and active celebrating of the wins, not to mention the increased morale and general happiness throughout the hotel.

You see, we all know how to do this. We did it when we were young and we do it when we play. As kids we are born with a natural instinct to persist, to ask and to have fun doing whatever it is we do.

I think we are all born as perfect SalesDogs. But then we get told things like "it's rude to ask" or "stop being silly" or "stop annoying others" or "sit down and be quiet." All of the things that we do instinctively—like speaking to strangers and shouting at the top of our voices just because we feel like it—are conditioned out of us.

I recently met a woman who told me that at her last parent-teacher conference for her five-year-old daughter she was told that her daughter was fine in school, but that she had "a little bit too much self-esteem." Can you imagine?

As we get scolded, punished, ridiculed or ignored, we get pushed back into a system of "seriousness"—especially when it comes to business.

Dogs will abandon their bones, their food and all their playthings for a good scratch behind the ears. They get super-excited the more you acknowledge them. Little kids do this too. Nothing has changed just because we are adults. Our brains and spirits are still the same.

This technique of celebration is foreign to most people, but second nature to high achievers. It also has to do with trapping the "little voice" and steering the dialogue in the right direction. And remember, it doesn't matter if what you are saying to yourself is true or not! Your body and mind do not care! Part of this dialogue has to do with how to make the event filter into all areas of your being and own it for yourself.

Handling success is the absolute opposite of handling setbacks. If something good happens, such as a prospect agreeing to an appointment or receiving any positive sign from the client, not only should you celebrate it as I mentioned, but to *really* build momentum you have to use it to become a Legend in your own Lunchtime!

Tell yourself that because of this success your whole week is going to be great. You can see how everything in your life is going to be successful just because of this tiny event.

Finally, it is important to internalize it by telling yourself that the success happened because of YOU. You earned it, you worked for it, you are smart and you know this stuff! Get the picture? Your energy and momentum will soar, and all SalesDogs know that the greater the energy the greater the next success.

You may not be aware of it, but you already know how to do this, because you did it with your kids, with your pets and with yourself in other areas of your life. When your kids were little, didn't you make a big deal and celebrate all of their new accomplishments? If your kid managed to stand, even for a split second, didn't you picture future Olympic glory? If you ever played golf, you've done this. Just as your frustration hits its peak and you're ready to toss your Pings into the lake, you knock a nine iron stiff, within three feet of the cup, or nail a forty-foot putt for birdie. What do you do? You clench your fist and give it the ol' Tiger Woods thrust and the frustration evaporates.

Imagine if you treated your whole life that way! Your energy and your results would be incredible. The problem is some people, even when they get a win, want to cut it off at the knees. They sink the putt and say to themselves, "Lucky that time." They make a successful call and say, "Too bad they aren't all like that." That is the dialogue that drives a spike into the heart of your spirit, your energy and your results. From now on, Be a Legend.

Bone for managers: Your pack of SalesDogs needs to celebrate their wins too! As a matter of fact, the smarter the breed and the more aggressive the dog, the more you have to bury them in lavish praise to ensure good performance. If neglected, or if only scolded for poor behavior, SalesDogs can get mean and nasty and may even turn on you one day. You must celebrate wins early and often to make them great hunters and companions.

For some reason, when we get older, go to work and take on careers, celebration become childish.

We are actually taught NOT to sell. We are taught NOT to ask. We are taught to work hard, be good, color within the lines and hope that someone will recognize us for our efforts and throw us some scraps. We are told that "all good things will come to those that wait." We are taught to accept, not object, to give, not to ask, and to accept our lot in life. We are manipulated and contorted to fit snugly into a ready-made box where we are expected to live quietly until we die. We are judged by our ability to answer questions, not ask them, and God forbid we should ever make a mistake!

I believe that everyone has the natural talent to sell. Every child can sell. You can sell. We are all born to sell. Some need more skills than others do. Some need a new attitude about it. Some are already hot on the hunt. The next time your kid pesters you for something, rather than telling him to knock it off, ask him to present you with at least three good reasons why you should act on his request. When you see those little eyes glance skyward in the search for solutions, smile to yourself and know that your training in this moment will be preparing him for a life of joy, love and wealth. And that is his birthright and destiny.

So celebrate, celebrate and celebrate some more. And by the way, a dog doesn't need a party or a raise to feel acknowledged or celebrated. A simple clap, pat, stroke or scratch of the neck will do.

SUMMARY

Wins are the most precious commodity you have. Most people have a natural mindset that minimizes them, but that is a killer of enthusiasm and energy! It is critical to learn how to spot the wins, trap them, own them, leverage them and save them for the next big event!

---

4. Project the Power of Your Personal Intention

The mastery of this technique is critical to forming a high-power sales team or organization. It is also the secret to reducing stress in the job, creating inspirational leadership and, most important, obtaining personal wealth. Learning how to project your intention of yourself and others can be the difference between frustration and riches.

Let me explain in dog terms. When a dog takes off after a

squirrel, a cat or a ball, it fully intends to GET IT! There is no "trying" involved, it is just doing. When they go up to you with their tongue hanging out and drool dripping on your shoes they fully intend for you to pet them. No question about it. That is their intention. If you as a SalesDog think that you are going to charm everyone you meet, you probably will do better than you think. However, if you think that you are going to be a nuisance to the prospect or that you are going to be boring— you probably will be! That is intention.

Learning how to project your intentions and expectations can be the difference between wealth and frustration. In other words, What do you expect the response to be from your next presentation? Will they think you are a rookie? Will they think that you are truly there to help them find new solutions? Will they like you, hate you, think you are a nuisance? What do you think that they will think? What is your intention?

Research shows us that whatever you believe the response is going to be will help to predetermine what the real response is! If you think that you are going to be a pest by making a sales call, you may very well be right. If, however, you think that you are going to be a welcome messenger of critical information, you may be right as well. Your mindset helps to predetermine the results.

Not too long ago, my son Benjamin (then aged four) had a dilemma. We were in Singapore during one of our overseas trips and we were staying in a serviced apartment complex in the city. We have stayed there many times because it has a great location and a big pool and there are always lots of kids for Ben to play with.

This place also has a game room with a pool table. Ben loves to play pool by rolling the balls without using the stick. The pool table requires two one-dollar Singapore coins. Ben knows this. On this day he had earned his two dollars by setting and clearing the table and was excited about playing pool later.

Before going to the poolroom we went down to the swimming pool to catch some sun and a little exercise. In typical SalesDog style, Ben spotted the soda machine and went for it and bought a Sprite and a Coke. Happy with his purchases he came back to Eileen and me with his goods.

We explained to him that he had just spent his pool-table money on the drinks. After a convoluted discussion that only a parent can understand, he was faced with the dilemma of two drinks that were now not nearly as desirable as his beloved pool table. A few moments later I heard a loud pounding sound. It was Ben trying to shove the cans of drink back into the machine in the hope of getting his money back!

After calming him down a bit, we made him realize that his only option was to somehow exchange the drinks for money. The light went on and you could see his little blue eyes survey his territory with laserlike precision—young couple, poolside, lock and load!

They had no chance! I do not know to this day if they even spoke English! He raced over to them, set the cans down and began his pitch. I could not hear anything, as he was too far away, but I watched in amazement. They obviously understood that he was offering the cans and that he wanted money in exchange. And judging from his gestures I think he was also explaining why he needed the money. At first they shook their heads, but his intention to sell those drinks was undeniable.

From the outset, there was no fear, no hesitation, no fear of looking foolish, only the pure intention to get them sold. I watched from a distance and laughed to myself. What a SalesDog! Ben had the mindset that he would not be denied. Finally, I watched in proud disbelief as they handed over the cherished coins. Ben even offered to open the cans for them so they could enjoy the drinks immediately (showing traces of the Retriever).

With coins in hand, he happily skipped back to us to tell us with delight of his accomplishment, leaving two refreshed customers in his wake.

That is intention!

He had no doubt that he would sell those things. Months later, he is still that way. He will persist and persist and never give up because he KNOWS that sooner or later he will find a chink in our armor and we will agree to his requests. All kids are SalesDogs.

BONES FOR MANAGERS REGARDING EXPECTATIONS AND INTENTIONS OF OTHERS

What is your expectation of your kennel? Whether you ever communicate it or not, that expectation will show itself somehow or other. Your intention or expectation of the performance ability of others will also partly predetermine their results. If you were to rank each of your SalesPups with a number from one to ten in terms of their potential for success, what would those numbers be? If you ranked someone with a three or four, you have already, in part, predisposed him or her to that level. It will show up in your management style and attitude and in their performance results.

Unfortunately, this also happened in school for many of us. Teachers hung invisible numbers on our foreheads. What numbers were hung on you? Did you believe them? What number have you hung on yourself? Is it helping or hurting you now? It is a rare SalesDog that overachieves what its master expects. Be careful of your intentions and expectations.

I had a salesman working for me in the airfreight business whom most other vendors and associates historically considered to be a pain in the b____t. He and I had a great relationship though, and within a short period he doubled our volume in one of our toughest and most competitive cities. I kept telling him that I knew he could succeed, even when he was whining and whimpering. After a while the sulking began to dissipate and was replaced by howling and celebratory yipping as one small win led to another and another.

This is a simple example of the effect a good Dog Trainer can have on a SalesDog—an example of a person who, because of his mannerisms, alienated lots of people. Every job that he held had produced mediocre results. He had drifted from job to job. He was a stray.

When I took him in, I started his training all over again. We identified him as a yipping Chihuahua that drove everyone nuts. We then trained him in the skills of the Retriever and the Basset Hound. His incredible Chihuahua mental quickness coupled with softness of tone and commitment to service made him one of the wealthiest salespeople in the territory. We celebrated wins, I acknowledged his efforts, and I told him I KNEW that he could make a ton of money. In other words, I believed in him even though others had taken the newspaper to him. The results spoke for themselves.

SUMMARY BONE FOR MANAGERS

Just as your intention affects your sales, your intention for your SalesDogs can limit them, or urge them to achieve extraordinary success. There is a number that ranks your expectations of others, yourself and your actions. If it is an expectation of others, it dangles right on that person's forehead and plays a large part in determining the level of performance that is achieved. It is most important that as a Dog Trainer, you shouldn't be prejudiced by limitations put on your SalesDogs by previous managers. Some of the scroungiest mutts make the best hunters, because their new master/trainer gave them a whole new expectation and perception of themselves. If you see them as champions, they will invariably rise to meet your expectations and become champions.

Training for the Hunt

FIVE CRITICAL SKILLS FOR
SALESDOG SUCCESS

For years, a classic argument has raged through sales confer-
ences, has been debated around water coolers and has inspired countless books: "Are great salespeople born or made?"

There is one school of thought that says that if you do not
have the assertiveness to make calls and handle objections, you
won't cut it in the long run. The other school of thought says
that everyone sells something and that depending on who you
are, you can be good at selling some things and not others.

This debate is as old as sales itself, but my heartfelt observation is this: Every child comes into this world learning to ask
for what it wants and needs. First for mere survival purposes
and then for things like love, affection, cuddles and later Poke-
mon, Playstation II and your car on a Saturday night!

Every child can sell. You can sell. We are all born to sell. I
believe that everyone has the natural talent to sell.

However, we lose that natural ability through conditioning and the seriousness of life. Most of us have been fed a ton

of conditioning about the evils of sales by those who lack the basic self-determinism to be able to say "No." They fear being manipulated and taken advantage of so they portray anyone who *does* sell as a money-grabbing, morally corrupt charlatan!

So to answer the question: "Are we born to sell?" I believe that we are all born great salespeople. But we lose the talent by the time we get to adulthood, so many of us must simply re-train what we already instinctively know.

It may be true that not everyone can sell everything. Not everyone can sell investments and not everyone can sell business machines. But based upon what breed you are you can sell something.

So now you know your breed and have learned to recognize the breeds of others. You now know the rules to follow to keep yourself out of trouble and in the money, and you are ready for the next step in your evolution.

To become the Blue-Ribbon Winner that you deserve to be, you must master the basic skills for SalesDog success.

The pooch that can't perform the fundamentals, like sitting, staying, rolling over, coming on command, fetching or playing dead—doesn't wow anyone. The same holds true for SalesDogs.

There are five critical skills that every SalesDog must master in order to be a great hunter:

1. Mastering the art of referrals.
2. Delivering powerful presentations.
3. Tapping the desire to serve others.
4. Managing the personal marketing versus selling formula.
5. Handling of objections or rejections.

Good SalesDogs are strong, committed and, above all, keep things "dog-simple." Remember, the maximum intellectual age of even the smartest dog is equivalent to that of a five-year-old child. It doesn't take much for them to make it to David Letterman's show! SalesDog tricks are just as simple but can end up producing tremendous results.

In other words, this is not rocket science!

1. Master the Art of Referrals

The number-one reason that people are intimidated by sales is the dreaded "cold call," so why not just avoid ever having to make them?

Dan Kennedy, one of the top marketing minds of the last decade and author of six books on the subject, stated it very well: "Why would you want to talk to anybody who doesn't already know you?"

Dogs are brilliant at picking up unspoken clues. It takes them all of about ten seconds to figure out if someone is a friend of yours. Once even a sniff of camaraderie is recognized, the tail starts to wag, the drool starts to flow and he is instantly nuzzling up to his newfound friend looking for a little affection!

Dogs don't wait for a formal invitation to get acquainted— they are making new friends all the time. Great SalesDogs, however, work best with an introduction.

While the Poodle can schmooze at parties and network on sheer instinct, and the Pit Bull can kamikaze the marketplace with a napalmlike barrage on anything with a pulse, the rest of the kennel are generally a little more subtle when it comes to the delicate art of referrals. There are four types of referrals. The first is the best kind. The quality of the referral decreases as you go down the list:

1. Friend gets prospect to call you—charm of the Poodle.
2. Friend tells prospect you will call him—easy for the Retriever.

3. Friend tells you who to call and allows you to mention that he or she referred you—Basset Hounds and Chihuahuas are comfortable with this one.
4. Friend gives you a name, any name!—good enough for the Pit Bull.

The key is that the introduction must include a personal endorsement—just one positive thing about YOU, not just the product or service you are offering. It doesn't have to be a dissertation or an epic biography, just a positive phrase about YOU! "John's a good guy." "You should listen to what Sally has to say, she really knows her stuff." "I trust Paul, he tells it straight."

This simple one-liner is critical because it gives you TRUSTWORTHINESS and initial RESPECT. These qualities are the secret ingredient to successful referrals. Like vanilla essence in the sponge cake—without them referrals will still work, but it won't be quite the same.

The bottom line is that people do business with people they like and people they trust. The product or service is often secondary. If you are already prequalified to fit into the "like" and "trust" category, then your chance of success has just skyrocketed. You are no longer the scrounging mutt or flea-infested nuisance that you would have been. You have just become a pedigree SalesDog and someone well worth taking a call from, and well worth actually listening to!

I have a friend who is in the real-estate business. He finds underperforming properties and remarkets them for profit. This requires an amassing of a large amount of investment capital to purchase these properties. To this day, I do not believe he has ever printed a brochure, made a sales call or even taken out an ad in a paper or magazine.

He has something even more powerful. It's his list of investors, all of whom were referred to him over the years. He sells his projects to investors without ever needing to approach someone cold. He and his wife are extremely wealthy and live in a beautiful home with their kids. Their success and their business are built purely by referral.

Personally I generate hundreds of thousands of dollars in speaking and training fees alone and 90 percent comes from referrals. I have spent tens of thousands of dollars on advertising and promotion. My return on that investment is terrible in comparison to the return on investment I get by making sure my existing customers are happy with their training results.

The ultimate referral is the quality of your reputation. It speaks for itself.

Investing time with your existing customers will usually generate ten times the rewards of other activities. Check in with them on a regular basis to make sure that they are happy and performing well, and referrals will snowball until you have so much business you can't keep up.

REFERRALS ARE EVERYTHING

There has never been a successful network marketer who did not understand the importance of referrals. If you are a person who puts money in other people's pockets by training them, coaching them and encouraging them, people will find you.

One of my dear friends markets an entire educational program through network marketing. His reputation for providing the finest training in his entire region has people flocking to him and his people. They know that they will be given the tools to help them be wealthy not only financially but also emotionally and spiritually. His business has grown at a rate of thousands of subscribers per month!

REFERRAL AND TESTIMONIAL ETIQUETTE

For those of you with Pit Bull in the blood, make sure that, if you are going to hound someone, you don't bother the potential prospect. He doesn't know you yet and it won't take long for you to burn up the benefits of the referral and get demoted back to nuisance scavenger status with all the other dogs on the block.

Instead, hound the person who promised to give you the referral, because he already has the rapport with the prospect and he already knows you and, one hopes, likes you! And he has already agreed to make the referral for you and will feel duty bound to keep that commitment.

Keep reminding him how much you will appreciate him for passing a referral to you. You can casually prompt him with: "Have you called so-and-so yet?" "Would you like me to get you his number?" "I didn't want to call him until I knew that you had called him first."

Make asking for and seeking referrals part of your Sales-Dog mindset and you will never have to sell cold to a stranger again. But remember it's a fine line between requesting help and becoming a pest. You need to carefully manage your referral streams, taking care not to poison the waters. If they think you are a nuisance, why would they ever send you to their friends?

However, the great thing about SalesDog training is that once you become adept at picking people's breed you can also use that information to tailor your communication so that you speak their specific language.

For example, say your existing client, John, is a Poodle and you would like to use him as a referral to a new prospect, named Steve. Remind John how grateful Steve is going to be to him for his advice and how Steve could be a great contact for his business at some future time.

On the other hand, if John were a Chihuahua, that approach wouldn't motivate him at all. Instead you would need to play on his thirst for knowledge. Tell John that Steve really needs to understand from a user's perspective the features and applications of your product or service and that you know of no other person who understands it better than John. You are looking to John to help Steve find an amazing product that will really help Steve's business. John gets to look like the expert.

Once you start to recognize the breed in people you can push their specific button. And it becomes a win/win/win. You win because you have the referral, the referral wins because you will help him or her by providing a valuable product or service and the client wins because he or she gets to feel good about making the referral.

There should also be a tangible reward to your customer for a successful referral. It could be a simple thank-you note, a bunch of flowers, a book or treating him to lunch. The best reward you can give is returning the favor and sending a good referral for his business.

When you are first getting started, sometimes it's hard to

get referrals. This is the time to tap your closest resources to get things going. Get your good clients, friends or associates to write you some glowing letters of support and satisfaction.

If they are too busy, you write the letters and simply have them read and sign them. Keep a collection. Make copies and when you want to call on someone new, send him a handful of appropriate letters as an introduction. If possible, choose letters that the person will relate to—letters from someone in a similar industry or business. Although you are not technically being referred by someone he knows, you are being referred by people you know, which adds credibility to your pitch. And you are proving that you have helped people like him in the past.

But be careful—testimonials can be used to your detriment. My wife and I were in the market for a new car a few years ago and went to the BMW dealership in our area. The salesman was very quick to pull out a thick notebook of letters of endorsement for himself and his firm. He simply plopped it down on his desk and said, "Here is what my customers think of me." Eileen and I looked at each other and smiled, knowing that there would probably not be a letter from us to go into that book. That is how NOT to use testimonials.

It's also extremely important to treat referrals with a deeper sense of service and commitment. This comes naturally to the Retriever, but can be a challenge for the Pit Bull. If you receive a referral from a client or friend, it's critical that the referred prospect has a good experience. This isn't the time for a hard sell or high pressure or it will quickly get back to the person who gave you the referral and it will be the last referral you receive from your contact.

However, if you can come up with an excellent solution to the referred prospect's needs, you might very well end up with another key source of referrals. And now the endorsement gains even more momentum. "I was referred to him and it was the best thing that ever happened to me. I highly recommend you do the same."

How hard are you going to have to sell this prospect? Hand him the pen and watch him write the check. The fact is that people don't like to waste time shopping around and being subjected to dozens of sales pitches. They would much rather get a good recommendation from a friend who can help with a good, trustworthy solution. By the time they talk to you, the walls of doubt and mistrust are down, and they are able to clearly hear the value of your offering.

By the way, to use testimonials or referrals, you do NOT have to come from pure bloodlines or royalty. Every SalesDog has had his or her day in the sun. You have made others ecstatically happy in the past. It's important to spend time documenting your victories. Blow the dust off some of your greatest wins and request testimonial letters from those clients. Often you can recall comments they made to you and put them down on paper. Many clients prefer that you actually write the letter for them, as long as you give them a chance to read and endorse what you have put down on paper.

If you are a new pup, use testimonials directed at your company, your sales manager or your industry. Though not as powerful as personal testimonials, they can be effective as well. The prospect probably won't read them anyway.

In his best-selling book *Influence*, Robert Cialdini talks of the six basic principles of psychology that direct human decision-making. They are reciprocity, consistency, social proof, liking, respect for perceived authority and scarcity.

If you build up a solid bank of testimonials and referrals you automatically appeal to three of these powerful principles—you prove that others agree that you are good (social proof), you prove that people like you (liking) and you prove that you know what you are doing (authority). The volume of material adds credibility and makes you a known quantity before a prospect even meets you.

Don't know where to turn to get a referral? Ask your best customers whom to call upon. If you are new to a territory, contact long-standing existing clients and ask them if they know of someone in need of your services in your new area. Some of your clients and friends might be extremely well-connected, and they often will be more than willing to plug you in to their system. They know that at one point, they had to start from scratch as well.

Remember it is an energy business. The more you network, the more you will get things rolling.

> **Bone: Never jump on strangers.** Contrary to the advice given in basic sales training courses, NEVER ask new clients for a referral until they are settled in with the product or service and you know they are satisfied. Asking for a referral right away may give them buyer's remorse. They will think that you are only interested in sales and not the relationship.
>
> **Big bone:** NEVER EVER EVER NEGLECT EXISTING CLIENTS. They are the greatest source of add-on sales, testimonials and referrals that you have.

2. Master the Ability to Deliver Powerful Presentations

It is a well-known fact that public speaking ranks higher than death in the list of top ten fears. However, if you want to be a

Champion you *must* master this skill. As with everything in life, the rewards for doing what other people can't or don't want to do are huge!

I have lived and profited by this very fact. There is much more leverage in talking to one hundred people than to one person, especially if you are introducing a product, service or business opportunity. Today in the education business I work in, 90 percent of my sales come directly from inquiries and leads generated from seminars and talks that I have done.

When I sold computers for Burroughs, I gave more seminars than anyone in the region and had the most sales. I did very few cold calls. Instead I promoted a "FREE one-hour seminar with refreshments" in a letter and fax campaign and newspaper ad and put on the show. All attendees would then know exactly who I was before I made a call to them.

More important, because I was the speaker, I became known to them as an "expert" and my advice carried a great deal more weight.

This combination of product information, education and FREE refreshments gave all the attendees a tremendous sense of value AND gave me credibility and authority in everything I then did.

It is critical that you know how to do this well, otherwise you become just another hound dog howling out of tune into the night. The great breeds attract their quarry and enroll them with charm, precision and control.

Some SalesDogs back off here and claim, "Well, I am not good at speaking to groups." My answer to that is, "Learn how now!" Speaking well is the most powerful sales tool you can have. If you ignore it, your income will suffer. Besides, if you are a true SalesDog, once you learn the SalesDog way of presenting, you will love it! That's a promise.

The ability to communicate confidently in front of people

not only enhances your own confidence but presents you as a credible authority, a leader. You become the one everyone wants to talk to because you're the expert, you're the one with the answers. The leader commands authority regardless of whether he is actually a good leader. And this is an extremely valuable perception to have on your side when you approach a prospect.

Unfortunately, most speakers are either yipping Chihuahuas talking bits and bytes at a hundred miles per hour, monotone, scarcely coherent Basset Hounds droning on endlessly, or self-absorbed Poodles trying to be cute, clever and witty. Most prospects can sense impending boredom at a hundred paces and "check out" within minutes. To be an effective speaker, you must have a diverse skill set,

HOW WELL CAN YOU PRESENT?

borrowing the best from each of the breeds. You must also develop important speaking skills in order to hold your audience.

Some say it is OK if you get 15 percent of the audience interested. Humbug! Your goal is to enroll 100 percent of the audience every time. You want to have everyone interested in talking to you further, wanting to buy from you, wanting more information from you or just plain excited about the experience of hearing you.

And this is how you do it:

EARN THE RIGHT

Who are you and why are you different? It is critical that you learn how to earn credibility quickly, easily and indisputably if you are to make dynamic presentations. Sometimes a deep look into your past can uncover gems that will instill confidence and respect in the minds of all of your attendees. These are experiences that tell the group that you know what you are talking about without boasting.

ASK FOR RESPONSES RATHER THAN TELLING

A friend of mine said it well: "Selling is not TELLING." Most presenters spend so much time telling everyone about the incredible data that they have they don't stop to contextualize that data for the audience by explaining exactly how it is going to benefit them. Selling is the art of asking the right questions to generate interest, create the process of discovery, build rapport and truly demonstrate your interest in the prospect. There is a particular art to doing this with a group. Believe it or not, the bigger the group, the easier it is.

ACKNOWLEDGE OTHERS

The key to a powerful presentation is obtaining active and passive participation on the part of the attendees. Once that is accomplished, you are in a working dialogue that leads to further discovery, rapport-building and interest. You must know how and when to acknowledge your audience and when to invite them to share their experiences in a way that raises the probability of sales. Without this interaction the presentation is dull, boring and very one-sided. Done poorly, it sounds like patronizing schmoozing, which is liable to backfire. Performed with skill and precision, it can put thousands of dollars in your pocket.

IDENTIFY AND CONFRONT SILENT ISSUES

It takes a bold and courageous SalesDog to do this but the benefits are massive. Have you ever noticed that well-trained dogs have no problem letting you know when they are hungry or when they need to go outside? They tell it like it is and pull very few punches.

Good presenters should be able to sense the mood and energy of a room. If they sense skepticism, confusion, doubt or any negative vibration, rather than glossing over it, they should address it immediately and directly.

"I get a sense that there is some doubt about what I am saying. Who would care to say how they feel about the information that I just delivered?" The energy of the room jumps up and the feeling of being disconnected from the group begins to subside. This is extremely valuable because you are addressing objections before they build up against you. Far too many presenters make the mistake of avoiding this confrontation and end up losing their audience.

LISTEN

Listening is obviously a critical skill in sales, yet few people are good at it. The listening ability of dogs is at least twenty-five times greater than that of the average person. They can pick up the sound of a snapping twig, the rustle of a rabbit in the brush at fifty yards or the operation of a can opener behind closed doors. Your SalesDog ears should be just as sensitive.

In a presentation it is important to focus and listen to what participants have to say ALL THE WAY THROUGH. The *natural* tendency is to try to gauge the intent and nature of the question as fast as you can and be ready with a good answer. While this is admirable and efficient, *this is the very reason most*

people are such poor listeners. The moment your mind begins to ponder an answer is the moment you stop listening. Like a dog's, your brain is not naturally conditioned to do too many things at one time. If you listen and stop thinking of the next witty comeback while someone is talking, two things will happen:

First, you will build an incredible connection with the person speaking, because he will sense your focus at both a conscious and subconscious level.

Second, you will hear valuable information about the person's emotional concerns and thoughts on the issues being raised. The most important part of any conversation is revealed at the end of a person's comments. So if you have "checked out" in "intellectual-land," you will miss the real selling signals! These critical elements of feedback are where the clues, hints and insights are hidden. And it is these gems that will allow you to ask specific questions in order to address the client's needs. Listening well also develops a more trusting and respectful relationship, which will encourage a positive buying decision.

ASK AND SOLICIT LOTS OF QUESTIONS

Whether you are presenting in front of a group or are in a one-to-one interview, you must continue to ask questions and encourage your audience to do the same. It is in this process that prospects' interest is developed, the relationship between the speaker and the participants is built and a working dialogue begins. Once started in a presentation, it becomes easy to request an appointment or meeting because it becomes simply a natural continuation of your conversation—a new chapter, not a new book.

TURN FEATURES INTO WHAT'S (SPECIFICALLY) IN IT FOR ME? (WIIFM) BENEFITS

Every basic sales training course tells you that customers make their decision to buy based upon the perceived benefit of your product or service. They will never buy features unless they are made relevant to their needs.

Do NOT use your time in front of the audience to simply list features and technogadgetry. It's a deadly mistake to assume that anyone will bridge the mental gap between a feature and the benefit it provides him or her. That's your job. YOU HAVE TO TELL THEM! This must be done with every claim, feature and item that you speak about. "This insurance policy has an increasing cash value. This is important to you because you can borrow from it tax-free in the future and thus reduce the money that you pay in taxes each year without reducing your actual income."

We have developed a unique SalesDog presentation program—both in live seminars and in a sales training kit—that aims at providing specific techniques and strategies based on the core strengths of each of the breeds. It will be the best investment that you will ever make in terms of catapulting your ability to make a sales presentation that will enroll, inspire and motivate prospects to be "wowed" by your presence and to buy only from you. I have literally watched people "transform" right before my eyes, as they test out these new presentation techniques.

And remember, you don't have to fill Madison Square Garden first time up! Start small and hone your skill.

3. Tap the Desire to Serve Others

Even the fiercest breeds of dog have an inborn desire to serve their masters. It is no mistake that dogs are the animals chosen to be aides for the blind and to be trained for police work. They are trained to track down travelers in distress, to find missing items, to deliver important messages and even to comfort the sick and feeble. Dogs serve their masters in part because of training, but more because of an innate desire to serve and to please.

While the strength of the Pit Bull, Terrier and other working breeds is to forge new territory and explore new and potentially hostile frontiers, the strength of the Golden Retriever is simply, and quite powerfully, its natural desire to please its master. The Golden Retriever SalesDogs' high level of service is directed toward their clients and prospects. Retrievers do whatever it takes to serve their clientele so fervently that it makes it very difficult for their prospects to say "No." While a Pit Bull will try to snatch a sale, the Retriever works from an entirely different angle. In a way, their clients feel *obligated* to give them the sale.

The Retriever knows, as do most dogs, that loyalty has its rewards. Dogs have been known to serve their masters in extraordinary ways. We've all heard tales of how these canine friends have defended seniors, rescued children and, at times, have even sacrificed their lives to save their masters'.

The desire to please, to serve and to protect is innate in every great canine companion. Great SalesDogs will not be successful unless they learn to hang out that tongue, develop a low whining sound and be patient enough to stand panting waiting for the next possible opportunity to serve their prospects.

A very successful friend of mine who is a realtor in Denver says it this way:

> I focus on customer service for several reasons. First
> of all I need to make a game out of what I do. I am

not the "cold-calling, ballbreaking" type of realtor. I work so much with first-time home buyers that it is easy to be a Retriever with them. I found that most buyers and often sellers are very uneducated in the home-buying/selling process. Many agents wouldn't care as long as they got the sale. I won't operate that way. I want sellers and buyers to have a good experience with real estate. I found that if I focus on customer service I have more ways of keeping in touch with past clients and thus referrals from them.

For example, I send out a copy of their appropriate closing documents (so they don't have to dig them up) that they will need for their accountant to do their taxes. I put together a notebook for buyers and one for sellers. It has pictures of my office with a history, lender information, a section on myself, how to reach me, etc., marketing techniques, my customer service in writing, copy of contracts, net sheet, the home buying or selling process and so on. I find that buyers seem to like these notebooks the best. They carry them around whenever we get together. I guess bottom line I like to keep in touch with past clients and use them as a source of business. Most clients tell me I'm more like a friend.

It's important to note that this advice comes from a VERY successful Retriever.

Sales is about taking the time and care to discover what someone really needs and then finding the solutions to that need. I have seen many accomplished salespeople with great initial numbers, great technique and great command of the product and the industry fail because they didn't *care* anymore and had no capacity to serve. They became demoralized and upset as their numbers dropped. Sadly, without addressing their problem they move on to other companies or products or territories, only to produce the same gut-wrenching roller-coaster results. This is one of the greatest risks of being a pure-bred Pit Bull. These attack dogs have a very difficult time realizing that a sale is just the beginning, not the end of a customer relationship.

I remember a very ambitious and highly talented guy named Fred who could charm the socks off anyone. For his first year selling insurance for a large, well-known firm, he broke every record. He was awesome.

Somehow, after that first year, his sales plateaued and then began a steady decline. He pushed hard, put in a ton of effort and time, yet he could not seem to replicate his rookie performance. He had no repeat business while others sold bigger and bigger policies to their existing customers. Frustrated with his results, he assumed that it was the insurance business that was the cause of his problems and decided to look for an alternative industry so he could rediscover his initial success.

A good friend turned him on to a very hot network marketing opportunity. Once again his numbers took off as before, but within months he had reached the same plateau. This time, however, his director spent some time observing and coaching him.

His director asked, "How much time do you spend with the people you enroll?" Fred's answer was typical: "I spend enough time for them to understand the program and then I look for more sales." Fred's problem was that he was focused on pure sales. His chief concern was how much he could sell and how fast he could sell it.

He committed very little of his time to support those that he had introduced to the program. This was the same problem that he had in insurance. In fact, he could barely remember why any of his clients had ever bought from him in either business.

Luckily for Fred, his director was a skilled Dog Trainer. He gave Fred an assignment. He was to go back and talk to every client he had ever sold insurance to and every person he ever enrolled and ask them why they purchased and what value they saw in the products. Fred was angry. "That will take forever! If I do that I will never make any sales!" Nonetheless he complied.

After a couple of weeks he sat down with his director again, this time with his tail between his legs. This was a new Fred.

He learned about the anguish and hope of a young family striving to make ends meet and to protect their future. He learned about how a simple marketing opportunity had taken one of his customers from rags to riches. In the process, he uncovered a wealth of information, insight and glowing testimonials. The stories were always there, but he had never taken the time to listen.

Fred's sales skyrocketed after that, and since then he has created his own network marketing company and is making millions. He tells all of his marketers, with whom he conducts regular training sessions, to simply look for a way to serve the customer. Even if your product can't do it, help them find a way to accomplish their goals. His favorite expression is, "Trust me . . . the service road becomes the fast road!"

Who says SalesDogs can't learn new tricks.

It is critical for all SalesDogs to ask themselves whom they want to serve and why. You must be willing to jump through hoops, over logs, through rivers and streams in order to bring back to your clients whatever it is that they need, want or desire.

There have been times I lost sales in order to accommodate the true needs of the customer. I lost sales, but never lost those customers, and I made up those momentary losses with bigger sales later on. All because I was willing to serve their needs first. That has got to be the passion! The Retriever knows this at a molecular level.

I once had a prospective client company that wanted to take on some project management training for some of their managers. I spent several long sessions and exchanged several lengthy proposals with them to try to satisfy their needs. At some point, it became apparent to me that I did not have the right program for them.

I told them that, as much as I would love to take on the account and find a way to offer them training, it was just not the right fit. I spent the next several weeks interviewing other potential candidates for them. I sat in on meetings, made phone calls and offered half a dozen choices for them. They finally selected one of my recommendations.

They never forgot the service I provided. A year later they called me to say that another division wanted a bit of team-building training and asked if I was interested. Of course I was, and that return phone call resulted in an ongoing eighty-thousand-dollar-a-year contract that I have had for five years.

The definition of sales IS NOT simply getting someone to buy. Sales IS making someone's life better in some way. That is service!

Sales manager bone: To inspire your SalesDogs you have to continually remind your pups of the service that they are providing to others. You can never overemphasize this. You must touch their hearts so that they will do the same with their prospects. That is where all meaningful decisions are made.

4. Manage the Personal Marketing Versus Selling Formula

Probably the most valuable skill to learn is how to market yourself effectively so that you do not have to sell at all!

For you Pit Bulls, who like nothing more than ripping up and down your territory looking for anything warm, this is contrary to your basic instinct. Your form of marketing involves picking up the phone or walking through the front door. So you might be tempted to skip this section.

But for the rest of you SalesDogs, and the now-curious Pit Bull, if you want to work less and sell more, personal marketing will change your life! If you learn a few tricks of the Poodle, you might discover how simple it is to get tremendous results.

Earlier, I mentioned that the key to the referral process is that, if it is done correctly, you will never have to speak to someone who does not already know you. That is called advance marketing, and here is what it can mean for your sales. There is a very simple formula:

$$S/M = \text{Sales Effort}$$
$$(S = \text{Sales}, M = \text{Marketing})$$

It's simple math: The more marketing you do, the less selling effort you have to deal with. If you currently spend equal time selling and marketing your product or service, and then decide to invest twice the amount of time marketing yourself, your product or your service, then you will end up expending half the effort! The more quality effort you spend marketing, the less you have to physically sell. Prospects put up their hands and come looking for you instead of your having to sniff them out.

Sales effort is physical, time-consuming, fraught with objections and requires great personal skills and time management. Marketing is leveraging your message to as many of your target prospects as possible without your physically having to do it yourself. Develop a set of marketing strategies, test them and execute them, and the sales will come to you rather than your chasing the sales.

It doesn't matter how many sales calls you make: You will never get to as many people as a well-placed headline in a trade journal aimed at your target market. Nor will you ever be able to compete with a website that is receiving thousands of hits a day.

Another formula for those who have trouble with the math:

$$\textbf{S (Sales)} \times \textbf{M (Marketing)} = \textbf{\$Results}$$
$$\textbf{(Double ``M'' and spend half the time on ``S''!)}$$

It's critical to learn how to balance your week between actively selling in front of live prospects or customers and

How Good Is Your Marketing?

developing a referral stream through your marketing efforts. If you are a wise SalesDog, you should spend quality time on your marketing strategies. Basically, it's the art of having sales opportunities come to you. And perhaps even more important, it's the process of increasing the odds that leads will convert to sales.

Unfortunately, there are packs of wild, untamed Sales-Dogs who prefer to run around chasing anything that moves. They spend the bulk of their time in pursuit of elusive prospects—catching few and burning themselves out in the process. The result is a meager income and an emotional flood of rejection and frustration.

You can have an easier, happier sales life. But to do so, you must learn how to market effectively!

Think about it. Rottweilers or Dobermans need no introductions; they thrive on their reputation. When 130 pounds of muscle and teeth appears, everyone has an expectation, an opinion and a short course of action. This image helps them in their roles as guard dogs, but leaves the average prospect quaking in his boots!

How many times have you walked to the other side of the street to avoid a confrontation with one of these potentially lethal dogs? Your prospects are no different. If you are overly aggressive, they will never come to you. In fact, they will avoid you!

How do your prospects perceive you? Not only do you need to market your product or service; you need to market yourself. You want people to have a good perception of you. You want them to think, "Here is someone who is going to help me solve my problem."

This is exactly why it is essential that a SalesDog must spend a lot of his or her time marketing himself or herself.

Good marketing, such as ads or links on websites, a well-placed headline in a trade journal, a best-selling book that refers to your services, will sell more than you ever could by just knocking on doors. By using media that are seen by hundreds or thousands, you are in essence knocking on the door of everyone who sees them. In addition to other media, you can use other speakers, other businesses, other organizations and any entity that is exposed to those who could be potential clients of yours to get your message out effectively.

Start by making a list of potential avenues you can use to

get the word out about you and your product. Spend time on developing those avenues and sales will happen automatically.

Second, be sure that whatever you send out for public exposure offers a compelling reason for someone to call you or to show interest. It should not be a billboard of your service. It must be an offer for a reward to them if they contact you. It can be a special offer for service, a fantastic guarantee, an irresistible yet truthful claim or simply a unique proposition.

A simple example could be to advertise a free consultation service or a limited-time discount or a "special free report" on competitive equipment if they call, fax, enroll or inquire.

Now keep it in mind that this is completely separate from the global marketing that your company is already doing for you. This is a much more personalized and direct marketing effort that will not only draw them to your product or service, but direct them to you.

Marketing is simply getting your prospects excited and educated about you and your service before you ever make a sales call. Because their interest is piqued, you are that far ahead of the game. Here are some avenues to get you started. There are thousands more.

- Create cooperative relationships with other individuals or companies that are already in contact with your prospects.
- Send out sales letters.
- Create compelling headlines and unique selling propositions to place in journals, magazines and print media and on websites.
- Advertise.
- Volunteer at industry functions.
- Fax blitzes to groups and prospects.
- Work trade shows.

- Conduct free educational seminars.
- Cosponsor community activities.
- Generate testimonials and referrals.

The problem is that most salespeople do not want to spend the time, money or effort necessary for marketing. They would rather be cheap and rely on their own physical endurance or wait for the company to do the marketing for them. Those who cannot or will not market a service or product can never move to the CASHFLOW B (business) quadrant. It takes the will to test, to make mistakes and to be corrected.

Think like a DOG. Sniff out the places that other human noses can't detect. If your nose is weak, work with others who are either in with the prey or have better noses. That is marketing.

While still in the computer business, I took over a territory with quite a few customers who had been using automated posting machines for years. Knowing that it would take ages to call on all of those clients, I got to know the field engineer in my territory, Masa, who did all of the repairs and preventive maintenance on those machines. Masa was a great guy who had been in the territory for more than twenty-five years!

He and I had coffee every Monday morning and we talked about the users. From those conversations we came up with a plan. Whenever he saw one of the users, he would casually mention to them the newer equipment that was available. He would point out the benefits these newer models offered, including less down time and lower maintenance costs. By the time I got to them, they were prepared, educated and eager to learn more. Masa had warmed them up and they were ready to go.

Within less than a year, I had replaced nearly all those aging units with state-of-the-art minicomputers. My area became the number-one territory in the entire United States for two years straight, simply because I spent more time marketing than I did selling. Masa won big too, because he was rewarded with additional commissions for new service contracts. We had forged a marketing partnership that made us both winners.

5. *Master the Handling of Objections or Rejections*

Certainly the biggest obstacle and the largest turn-off to becoming a salesperson is the rejection. Nobody likes it! We all want to be loved and accepted, so rejection is not something most of us like.

Dogs also love to be loved and accepted but they don't take it personally when you do not have the time to throw the Frisbee with them. As a SalesDog you must learn to react the same way. Later chapters talk in depth about how to handle rejections, but here are some key points:

1. The objection that a prospect gives you is not the problem. It is your emotional response to the objection that is the problem. Once you are able to remain emotion-LESS in the face of the hardest critique, your brilliant mind will be able to handle those situations with ease. The problem is that rejection stimulates our most primal fears as human beings and causes deep emotional and mental disturbance. Classic rules of communication say that when you are in a heightened negative emotional state, your intelligence is low. Have you ever said something when you were upset and later wished you'd never said it at all? Have you ever been rendered speechless when someone got upset with you, only to come up with a snappy comeback hours later after you'd cooled off? That is what I mean.

2. The skill of being cool and calm under fire is extremely easy to learn and rarely taught. It starts by erasing your own emotional responses through repetition.

3. In the case of upset clients or prospects, you must learn how to identify the emotion behind their words. Once you do that, their objection begins to subside.

4. Know also that behind every objection lies a benefit. For example: The objection might be, "The kitchen in this house is too small!" but the benefit is, "We made the kitchen smaller in order to give more room to the living and entertainment area. This will keep people out of your kitchen when you are entertaining and in the other parts of the house."

Another technique that has worked wonders for me and other SalesDogs is the "magic wand" approach. When first interviewing a new prospect or when you receive too many objections, ask this question: "If I were to wave a magic wand in this case, what is it you would want or what is it that would work best?" This basic query repeatedly creates new avenues of possibilities and opportunity.

Bone: Don't take it personally. When a prospect says "No" all he is saying is that he is not interested in your product at this time or that he doesn't understand something. It is *not* a reflection on you.

12 Managing SalesDog Emotions

Part of the difficulty that comes with dealing with passionate, high-performance people is that they are often run by their emotions.

SalesDogs are under a great deal of pressure to perform. Management expectations, peer pressure, the genuine desire to win and financial pressure will combine to form a very potent and emotionally charged environment that must be managed with skill and forethought.

Have you ever seen a normally good dog sulking around the house, growling at everything that moves? SalesDogs are the same. As a great SalesDog, you have to know how to motivate yourself, especially when you just want to stop the world and get off!

You have to know that there will be good days and bad days. There will be days when you want to just howl at the moon, days when you will want to chew someone's ear off and other days when all you want to do is play and chase. As with dogs, it is important NOT to encourage negative behavior. Yet it is critical to understand how to deal with the range of emotions that you or your SalesDogs will go through.

Emotional mastery is one of the most valuable and essential skills any great SalesDog must learn. I have never seen a great SalesDog, a great performer, a great team or a successful individual who became great without pressure! It is only under pressure that inner resources can be tapped and the confidence and ability of the individual can flourish and expand. Pressure is the laser beam of excellence that will elevate you to a whole new level of possibility by building the neurological bridges from "I might," "I can," "I must" to "I did."

Never fear pressure—greatness was rarely ever forged without it.

Pressure is how nature evolves. It is how new structures are formed. It is how we grow as individuals, teams and civilizations. It is not always something to be feared or avoided. It also does not always have to be painful, if you understand how to work with it.

No matter how beneficial the end result is, the reality of pressure in the moment can cause discomfort and stress if you do not know how to deal with it. If you are a mentor, director, manager or SalesDog yourself you must find ways to release that pressure before it becomes harmful to either you or your team.

Without this release SalesDogs can become paranoid (think the company is out to take advantage of them), negative (rude and snappy at colleagues and clients) or depressed (sulking, lacking initiative, doomsdayish).

As a SalesDog, you have to first address the emotions in question before you engage in another activity, especially sales activity. Left unresolved, these concerns will hinder your future efforts and can snowball into further depression, anger and despair. In a profession where being upbeat and optimistic is critical for success, this despondent mood can prove catastrophic to your sales. And left unchecked it can spread through the entire kennel.

You can't "force" someone or yourself to be happy and positive. But one of the great advantages of being human is that we do have control over our own emotions, and we can find unique and creative ways to positively affect the way we feel.

When your emotions run low, change your state quickly. If you are experiencing an emotional low (you know . . . "nobody likes me," "the company sucks," "I'm not cut out for this," blah blah blah!), pick a strategy that gets you into action that will set you up for small victories. Go and call on a good customer or user of your product or service. Talk to people who already love you and your service. Visit them, hang out with them, and even grab a testimonial or two while you're there. You will find that your mood and energy will change quickly.

Get physical—go for a good long run or visit the gym! Go and sit on the beach and get connected to nature again. What about making a tape of all your favorite music? Lively, motivational dance tracks that get you pumped up and feeling good. Play it as you go to visit your customers and sing out loud in the car—have some fun and use your voice. You'll be amazed how energized and empowered you feel afterward. Get creative.

When you are on a high—when everything seems to work—you are in the zone. This is when you find money in your pocket, people open doors for you and everyone loves hearing from you or learning about your product. This is the time to make even more calls. Take full advantage of this Midas phase and call anyone and everyone you can. You will be surprised at your effectiveness and the amount of sales you will amass during these times.

Resist the temptation to kick back and rest on a win or two. You will lose the momentum and it may be very difficult to get it back. If you have to continually restart your sales effort from a standing start you will expend significantly more energy than if you just keep it going—never allow it to stop. Keep moving and milk those highs for as long as you can.

Bone for the managers: As a SalesDog manager it takes a great deal of finesse and skill to help your pooches enter a more healthy and resourceful frame of mind. Owners who scold their dogs and then keep scolding them after the incident end up with nasty animals. With your SalesDogs you have to move quickly. Address the issue and then let it go! Don't let your anger or frustration linger or you will just make matters worse and you risk breaking their spirit and losing their loyalty.

At the first sign of moodiness, pull your SalesDogs aside and encourage them to let you know what is on their mind. Through their response, attempt to identify the actual emotion involved. You often need to dig deeper than their initial feedback. Remember what we said earlier about listening—listen all the way through. You will probably find that the real issues will start to emerge right at the end of the discussion. If you have "checked out" because you think you know the problem and are now thinking of a creative solution, chances are you won't hear the real issues being voiced.

"You don't seem yourself today, Sarah, you seem *depressed.*" "You appear to be a bit more *negative* about things than usual."

By doing this you have acknowledged the emotion and will automatically raise their emotional state of mind. (This is exactly what a counselor does when you go to a therapy session.) The simple act of acknowledgment shows that you care and that you are aware that there is a change in their behavior.

As they share their concerns, resist the temptation to offer knee-jerk advice, justification or counseling. Simply listen, acknowledge their issues and tell them that you can understand how they feel under the circumstances. After they have opened up, ask them some specific questions aimed at helping them arrive at a positive solution.

"What *has been* working for you lately, Sarah?" "What hasn't been working?" Ask them about new trends that are developing in their territories, their line of business or their industry. But be careful not to make it a twenty-question session that makes them feel inferior or under attack. The object of this exercise is to get your SalesDogs to think about specifics.

When things go badly we have a tendency to use the universal descriptors we mentioned earlier, such as, "Nothing *ever* goes right," "This is *always* a disaster." If you can ask specific questions it shifts the perception, allowing them to see that it isn't in fact *always,* just *sometimes.* Then if you can isolate enough *sometimes* you can change the behavior and avoid the frustration. This also acts as a kind of brainstorming session, and often solutions start to present themselves just through discussion and feedback. The energy then shifts to a more positive level and suddenly things don't look so bleak and action plans for success can be formulated.

With this approach we move from "this is *always* a disaster" to "well, actually it only seems to happen when I don't send the proposal within twenty-four hours." The solution is then obvious and you have a system and strategy that can be tested and measured in the future.

After listening carefully, work with them to develop a plan for success. It's important to break the "future victory" into small, attainable steps so that they can work themselves back to the right frame of mind and take ownership of that process so they realize that it is *them*, not *you* making the difference.

Like dogs, SalesDogs have trouble concentrating on too many things at once. If you throw sticks for the dogs, they will retrieve. It snaps them out of their slump because it is something fun to do. To further distract them, throw a second stick while they are retrieving the first one. That will totally take their mind off the original problem. Chances are they will drop the first stick to go after the second one.

That is why it is important for you as a SalesDog to get off onto some plan of action quickly that is fun, easy and distracts you from the current dilemma. Once your positive mindset has returned, you are ready to take on the world once again.

Here are a few action ideas to get that SalesDog moving:

- Find three newspaper articles that verify the importance of prospects' taking financial control of their lives.
- Get testimonials from four past clients. Find out and get excited about the positive difference you have made in their lives!
- Go talk to two users and ask them why they continue to use your product or service.

If it is a petty concern, let it go. But if you notice a trend of negative behavior, the worst thing to do is to ignore the emotion and try to brush it under the carpet or pretend it's not there and hope it will go away. Emotion is a good thing—it reminds us we are still alive! It is what generates passion and excitement. As a Dog Trainer, managing energy is the key to successful sales. When energy levels are high, so are sales. This process can also be used effectively to shift the mood of a client, prospect or customer and the SalesDog that is able to gradually and elegantly lift the energy level of a prospect will be a winning dog.

It is critical to understand that *you choose* the emotion that you want to have right now. The emotion that you choose to feel in any given moment shifts everything. It is not just thought. Emotion is much stronger.

Remember a time when you have walked in on two people, perhaps having an argument. You don't know what it was about but you can feel the emotion in the room: "You could cut the atmosphere with a knife." This is what other people pick up around you, so you have to be really conscious of all the unspoken nuances.

How do you want to feel? Angry, frustrated, excited, determined or optimistic? Do you like sensing anger from someone? What about depression—does someone need to say he is depressed for you to know, or can you feel that vibe from him before he utters a single word?

Emotion is generated through your focus. When you shift your focus you shift your emotions. When you need to shift your focus and get your emotions to start working for you instead of against you, try this (this takes only about one to two minutes):

1. What is it about this situation that you really don't like? Talk about it. Be specific—just saying "this sucks" won't work!

2. Then focus on what you want. Talk about it. Stay focused on what you DO want until you can see it, feel it, hear it and maybe even smile about it. THAT IS IT. Hold that feeling as long as you can. Repeat the process as often as possible. Remember, you don't have to come up with an action plan to get what you want, just stop focusing on what you don't want and concentrate on what you do want.

It's easy to do only step one! You probably do that daily. That is why most people end up with more of what they do NOT want. Step two is the most important part.

I had to make a presentation to a very large client recently. The contract in question was for over three hundred thousand dollars. I was nervous and concerned because I felt that the client was not going to be interested in what I felt was in his best interest. I fretted and complained to my wife, my associates and myself. I was angry and upset that the presentation was not going to go well. I was clear what I did NOT want. Normally, we leave our frustrations right there and end up having to struggle with our results, which are, very often, nothing more than a self-fulfilling prophecy.

In this case I chose to change my emotion and focus on what I DID want. I wanted to have an open discussion with the client and not a formal presentation. All I wanted was to have a lively conversation about his needs and my honest recommendations and to create a new and maturer relationship with the client. As I envisioned this conversation and began to feel what this new relationship would feel and look like, I began to smile and chuckle inside. It would be wonderful!

A day later I made the presentation, changed the relationship with the client and got rave reviews about our discussions. I have since embarked on a contract with him worth twice as much.

Had I chosen to be skeptical, frustrated, guarded or defensive, that new relationship would never have formed. I refocused on what I did want and got back on course to the positive outcome I wanted—and got it!

Part of the thrill of success in sales is knowing that there will be highs. Remember to anchor those highs and link them closer together. When the lows come, and they will come, simply refocus on what you want, employ the disciplines of action—any action to pull yourself out of the lows as quickly as possible. This will shorten the duration of the lows and keep you roaring back.

Bone: As SalesDogs, most of us are motivated by money, otherwise we would be administrative assistants in a local government department getting 1 percent pay increases each year! We are inspired by the limitless potential of our earnings. But is it really the money or is it what we want to buy with the money? When it comes to setting sales goals, focus on the numerical values only as a label. For real power and excitement, focus on what you will DO with the $$$. And focus on those things until you smile. I guarantee your energy will climb!

But it is important to remember that it never stays high and it never stays low. That is how nature works. Dogs know that even though it is raining and they are shivering outside in the wet and cold, sooner or later the rain will stop, they will find shelter and the sun will appear. The joy of selling is knowing that you will experience a range of emotion and passion nearly every day of your career, if you choose. A person who works hard to mask and hide emotion and who cautiously avoids the lows and the highs will not be an optimal SalesDog until he learns to express and experience his full range of feelings.

Mature SalesDogs take emotion and convert it into passion. Frustration transforms into determination. Anger and fear turn to power. Joy turns to pure optimism and unstoppable momentum.

How do you do this? Remember it is a conditioning process. Celebrate wins no matter how small they are. Tell yourself that you are a Legend even if what you have accomplished is no big deal. When emotional energy is low, engage in a high-activity endeavor that is fairly mindless but high-energy. Something like dropping off new flyers to prospects. Go for a run. Create a new marketing letter and test it on twenty people.

You have got to turn around the momentum in whatever way you can and distract yourself from the negative emotions. It's important, however, not to confuse "distract" with "ignore." You must identify and acknowledge the emotion that you have before moving on, otherwise it will simply resurface further down the track, only with even more momentum.

Don't hide your emotion. Understand it, give it a name, sit with it awhile, acknowledge it, release it and move on. Don't wallow in it. If you are comfortable with your emotions, you will know that you have a certain pattern of responses that you naturally go through, even from the lows. Anger can ultimately produce resourcefulness and determination. Disappointment may generate resolve. Know your pattern . . . if it is a good one . . . be patient. If it is a negative one, spot where you need to shift it.

The strength of a great SalesDog can also be his or her biggest liability.

The ability to take action is one that we can all benefit from, but it can be taken to extremes. Sales also requires patience. Too many times a dog takes off down another track because of impatience to get the quicker reward. This usually results in a very busy dog chasing so many rabbits that it ends up chasing its own tail. A good trainer disciplines the dog to stay on the track and hunt its prey down until the end.

So a good trainer must encourage her SalesDogs to be patient with the quiet times. You just have to keep the prospect funnel full; keep throwing in the leads and following up the calls and sooner or later a sale will pop out the other end. This is no time to abandon sound marketing strategy. When low emotional times settle in, patience and perseverance must work together. Like everything, it will cycle out again. That is why it is important to be sure that in your mind, all setbacks are Temporary, Specific and External. If you put that mindset into practice, you will recover from adversity in a fraction of the time and get back in the hunt for another day!

13

What Keeps Them Coming Back?

UNTOLD SECRETS OF HANDLING OBJECTIONS AND REJECTIONS

Big Kahuna bone: Of all the things that you can learn, the time you spend on the subject of handling rejections and objections is the most valuable. I can honestly tell you that if you train diligently in this subject your life will change. Not only will your sales increase, but you will find that the quality of your relationships will skyrocket. Most people have no idea how much their internal subconscious fears and concerns affect their conversations, actions and relationships with others, both at home and at work!

What is it about a dog that once they have decided to play fetch, they don't stop pestering you until you throw that ball? No matter how long it's been since you last played with them, they are as hopeful as ever that you will entertain them now. Dogs will sit there patiently while you read the paper or talk on the phone—all the time carefully studying your every move for the smallest sign of weakness or distraction so they can pounce!

You can tell them "Not now" or "Go away" but they just sit there—waiting. No matter how long you reject their efforts, even until the slobber has dried on the ball, dogs will never give up. Some will even block your path as you try to walk away to do something else. Why is this? What keeps them coming back in the face of rejection and setback? They don't realize they are being rejected and they don't understand when you tell them to go away!

Objections and rejections are the biggest obstacles for most SalesDogs. All the sales strategies in the world are worthless if you're a SalesDog that runs for cover the first or second time you are told to beat it.

Think about it. Do you have to sit down with dogs and coach them on their personal self-esteem? Do you have to give them complicated negotiation strategies for them to get people to throw the ball? I think not.

It's important to learn and practice the management skills I discussed earlier in the book. Celebrating wins and reinterpreting adversity is very important, but here is the real secret, the magic and wondrous mojo behind how all great SalesDogs handle objection and rejection.

THEY ARE USED TO IT!

I would love to tell you that there is an easier way, a quick fix that will make you immune without the time, commitment and pain, but there isn't.

This is the only way. The way out of fearing rejection is through experiencing rejection. You must experience objection and rejection in order to understand it, and you must move through it so many times that it simply doesn't affect you anymore.

The typical dog has been scolded and told off so many times that he is desensitized to it. He is numb to rejection, it's no big deal, been there, heard that, got the T-shirt and saw the video—now throw the damn ball!

The problem is that until you and your SalesDogs are used to it, their dainty poodlelike egos have a tough time coping with it successfully. Most people never encounter it because they are terrified of it and avoid it at all costs. The problem with that strategy is that if you avoid rejection you avoid sales and you are losing thousands of dollars a month in lost sales!

By the way, the "smartest" dogs (you know, the inbred, schizophrenic, high-strung, high-society dogs) sometimes have the hardest time with street selling. They have so little experience of failure in all aspects of their life that many can't stand the mere chance of being shot down in flames. Junkyard SalesDogs, SalesMutts and SalesDogs from the other side of the tracks can make the best salespeople sometimes, because they are USED TO DEALING WITH ADVERSITY. They understand that failure is sometimes part of life.

Of the entire kennel, this trait is the Pit Bulls' real claim to fame. They seem to thrive and look forward to taking objections just so they can snarl back some piercing and clever response. Which, by the way, is NOT necessarily the best way to handle objection.

It is a skill that once mastered will forever change your life in terms of your courage to take risks and to develop wonderful long-term relationships. Your ability to endure confrontation and disagreement will shatter the walls of fear, allowing you to go places others can only dream of.

Please understand this quality will not only make you rich in sales but will give you the courage to live your life your way. How many times have you said "Yes" when you meant "No"?

How many of us curb or change our personalities to fit other people's perception of us? How many of us lie to ourselves because it's "easier" than lying to others?

We are brought up with the notion that we must be everything to everyone. We must be accepted and loved and help everyone all the time. What about us? What happened to being true to ourselves, what happened to helping ourselves to be happy, what happened to accepting and loving who we are as individuals?

Until you can learn to stand up and be counted for who and what you are you will NEVER live the life of your dreams. You will live the life of other people's dreams. I can't explain the personal integrity, self-assurance and peace that will come to you when you know that no matter what someone says or does you are OK just the way you are.

So how do you learn this life-changing skill? Simple. To get accustomed to it quickly—immerse yourself in it by drilling in it. Drill and repeat the most common objections and rejections over and over again. There are about thirty commonly heard objections and rejections. These global objections can paralyze and intimidate most salespeople. With practice and repetition, you can dilute their impact and easily dispel the emotional charge each one carries. They become what they truly are, "No big deal!" (A sales training kit that can accelerate this process can be ordered at salesdog.com.)

When I first started to present to groups, I was both blessed and cursed by a group of friends who were attempting to develop the same skills at the same time I was. We used to lock ourselves in a room for hours and take turns standing in front of the room handling fictitious questions or objections.

We would hear stuff like, "What gives you the right to talk to us about this subject? You have never run a company as big as ours and probably have no clue!" or "You are just like all the rest of those stupid consultants who couldn't run a company so you decided to teach or sell instead."

A sense of decency will not allow me to print some of the other verbal artillery that was used during these sessions, but when people know each other that well, they can say some pretty nasty stuff, stuff that would leave even a frothing Pit Bull quivering.

To this day, I still vividly remember one such session. There were about ten of us stuffed into a room, and all of us were tired and testy after a long day of work in our respective businesses. It was quite a mixed group: One person was the owner of a large advertising agency, another owned a manufacturing operation and a couple of others were senior managers at large public companies.

On this particular evening, my friend John, the owner and sales manager for a top retail clothing and manufacturing firm, was preparing for a major presentation that was to be given the next day. John took his place at the front of the group and began presenting. Frankly, it was very dry, uninspiring and obviously not very well-rehearsed.

After just a minute or two the dogs were let loose and one of the senior managers began lobbing objections. "What's the point of this anyway?" Another added, "This is boring." While another chimed in quite bluntly with, "You have no idea what you are talking about."

John was clearly flustered, but to his credit he continued. He got louder and more arrogant and more upset as he went on, but not any more interesting. This only goaded the rest of us to attack even harder. (It was a brutal group. We were twenty times tougher than any prospect would ever dare to be.)

Finally, John had had enough. He abruptly gathered his notes and stormed toward the door. "I don't care what you guys think," he said. "It's my presentation and I'm going to do it my way!"

We all booed him as he made his way toward the door. But before he could exit, Karl, a senior partner in an international accounting firm and a guy who's six foot plus and more than 250 pounds, moved into the doorway. "You'll have to get through me if you think you can leave without facing the music and taking the correction," Karl said.

The room became dead silent. No one moved.

John stopped in his tracks: The gauntlet had been thrown down. John stared at Karl, looked back at us and started to laugh. "I was only kidding," he said. A cheer went up from the crowd as John resumed his place in the hotseat and launched into his presentation yet again.

We worked with him until he had it down to a fine art and the next day he blew his audience away. Believe it or not, John is now a best-selling author and an electrifying speaker around the world. For all of us, these experiences were truly transformational.

But interestingly enough, no matter how vicious the attack, after you have heard it enough times, it becomes banal. You just sail right past it on to the next question or the next piece of information. But best of all, the pounding in your chest that sounds so loud you can barely hear yourself speak and the perspiration running down your back simply fade away.

These drills are essential and I still do them to this day, either in front of a mirror or my wife, who willingly volunteers to tear strips off me for fun!

I have found that those who have drilled diligently have noticeably increased their personal sales because by the time they get in front of a real objecting customer, it is NO BIG DEAL!!

Dogs have real simple brains. They live in a world of instinct, loyalty and reward. Humans are a little more complicated, but we still have the same primal simplicity. In fact, recent studies have shown that when we perceive a threat our brains actually physically "downshift" from our higher-order logical thinking regions into the emotional, memory and even survival regions of the brain.

This makes logic and reason nearly impossible to access because your thinking process is being neurologically hijacked by the emotional and survival parts of your brain.

Most sales training philosophies emphasize the need for salespeople not to get defensive. Common wisdom tells you that once a person gets defensive, all he is going to do is turn off the prospect. This is great advice. However, defensiveness is a natural state of mind when you are under siege of rejections or objections. How do you overcome this?

The answer is a systematic reconditioning of your mind. Basically, you need to reprogram your responses. You clearly understand the common teaching that an objection is simply an avenue for further discussion, clarification or understanding. But without retraining your reactions, you will never be able to keep emotion from overwhelming logic and reason.

Note: Dogs, on the other hand, when perceiving a threat, either sniff it out in a sort of dumb curiosity or bare their teeth to defend. (A good SalesDog should probably choose the curiosity response. This is where your Pit Bulls will need a choker-chain every once in a while to battle their natural instincts.)

How many times can you recall when someone got really "in your face" about something, told you to beat it, or simply crushed your excitement? Do you remember standing there either fuming, perspiring or brooding, just wishing you had a great snappy, witty or maybe even cutting comeback? Instead you probably stood there and took it, mumbled some impotent comments and sulked away with the hair raised on the back of your neck or with your tail between your legs. Then, hours later, you finally came up with a great comeback! If only there was a "rewind button" when it came to sales and you could have another chance. Where was this great response to your prospect's objection when you needed it? The truth is it was there all the time, trapped under a heap of emotional responses.

Remember that the objection is not the problem. The issue is that the objection elevates your emotional response and reduces the ability to think clearly. The situation is further complicated because at the same time it is interpreted as a personal failure, leaving a psychic wound to the soul.

Once again, the way to get over this typical emotional meltdown is though repetition at responding to objections in a practice environment. Once you are properly desensitized, when real objections are getting fired in your direction, you can easily shrug them off and even smile inside knowing that "I've heard that one before!" You can then continue sniffing, asking, probing and pursuing with the relentless curiosity inherent in all great SalesDogs.

A key thing to learn from our canine friends is that no matter how many times you blow them off, no matter how many times you reject their attempts to nuzzle their nose into your lap for a friendly stroke, THEY NEVER GIVE UP AND THEY NEVER TAKE IT PERSONALLY!

Metropolitan Life Insurance and a team of psychologists studied the internal mental dialogue of thousands of salespeople. They learned that a proportion of these salespeople were skilled at interpreting rejection much as we described in Chapter Ten. They interpreted rejection as:

1. A specific nonrelated incident
2. Having no bearing on any other aspects of their life

3. Being caused by external factors such as timing, the prospect's mood or issues that the prospect was dealing with

Another group in the study had the opposite reaction to rejection. They saw it as a negative pattern that was reflective of other negative things happening in their lives. They reported feeling that there was something inherently wrong with them that was actually creating these negative results. Comparing the sales performance of the two groups, the results were startling. *The first group consistently sold over 34 percent more than the second group.*

Bone: SalesDogs has found a way to test for, and correct if necessary, those tendencies before a sales call is ever made (see the aptitude test at salesdogs.com).

There are a few dogs that, because of being beaten and abused, have very low self-esteem. The minute you raise your hand they cower in anticipation of being struck. Yet, even these dogs come back again and again for strokes of kindness. I don't believe that most dogs ever catch the cats they chase. Yet I have never seen a dog at the end of a chase crumple to the ground, putting its paws over its eyes and whimpering in disgrace. Instead their tongues are dangling, the drool is flowing and they are once again ready to continue the chase.

Remember above all: Never, ever take objections and rejections personally. During a sales encounter the blame must always be shifted elsewhere.

I am not saying that you shouldn't take responsibility for your

results. This doesn't mean you should be wasting time blaming outside forces and dreaming up conspiracy theories. I am simply saying that being responsible does not mean beating your head against the wall. It means not allowing a negative sales event to fester into a negative generalization about your entire life.

The thing to remember is salespeople are on the front line all day every day in support of their company. When a hand grenade tumbles into the foxhole, should you hold it in your hand and analyze why it's there? No. Get rid of it!

Learn from the encounter so that you don't get another one thrown at you. But don't sit and look at it till it goes off in your face.

You must draw from the experience and begin to develop winning formulas and patterns that will make you more successful in the future. You'll discover trends, such as, "Monday afternoons are a good time to call corporate executives," or, "It's important to be sure that all decision-makers are present at all important presentations," or, "Demos need to be short and sweet or you will lose the interest of your prospects."

I highly recommend that you take the objections from the SalesDog training kit (go to salesdogs.com) and drill them over and over with your colleagues and friends and by yourself. It is not important in the beginning to answer them. Just hear them and say, "Thank You," until you can do it without the element of emotion.

Then start to develop rational and logical responses to the questions and objections. You will be amazed how many valid answers there are to the same questions. In the beginning, you can use the quickie mindset techniques that we discussed earlier in the book. Once you go live, you will be so well-armed that you will actually find yourself hoping to hear your favorite objections! You will always be able to stay in the hunt and there will never be a need to run for cover.

The best way to react upon receiving an objection is by following the objection with good and honest probing questions. Snappy comebacks or questions designed to trap the prospect into agreeing with you only alienate the prospect. It must never be a contest between you and the prospect! This is a process in which you gently move the prospect to a point where he will allow you to be helpful.

Once you have successfully learned the technique of remaining calm and thinking clearly, you can take your development a step further. You do this by asking questions to get more information and clarification.

First, always acknowledge the objection with a "thank you" and then restate the objection to show that you truly listened and have understood.

"Now if I heard you correctly, I believe that you are saying that the timing of this installation is super critical to the whole project."

This shows that you understand your customer. If he agrees with your retelling of the objection, then ask some questions to further explore his concerns. Be sincere and avoid manipulative "why" questions. Your goal is not to prove his ignorance, but to have a clear understanding of the issues at hand.

Most salespeople try to turn the objection around to get immediate agreement from the customer. This ham-handed form of manipulation only angers any intelligent person. Stay clear of "buts and ifs." If you use those immediately after the objection, the prospect will know that you are trying either to argue ("I understand, but . . .") or to force him to admit to something ("If I showed you that . . ."). Your questions should be asking why he has particular problems in a way that shows empathy and genuine interest.

Another tip: Each SalesDog has its own nemesis. Some Pit Bulls get nervous around small animals or only like male companions. There are many Poodles that are terrified of large dogs. Large animals and strange sounds can spook Basset Hounds. Part of the way you get dogs to overcome their fear of other animals (SalesDog and canine) is to make sure they are exposed to their nemesis in nonthreatening, nonsales situations.

For some SalesDogs, intimidation comes in the form of older, gray-templed, sophisticated-looking white males who appear to have great authority. Some are troubled by aggressive female prospects. There are some older dogs who are even a bit miffed by young, cocky, arrogant pups. Experiment with different scenarios until you find the one that strikes the most intimidation in you. Drill the objections again and again and imagine your biggest nemesis barking the objection.

I used to be really intimidated by the stereotypical senior executive with gray hair, about six feet plus tall, dark-rimmed glasses, with very impatient looks. I would fumble for words all the time with such prospects. Until I got over my hangup with these executives, my ability to sell at senior levels of organizations was frustrating and only minimally successful.

When I began conducting seminars, it seemed that more and more of those types would show up and challenge me. I knew I had to handle it, so rather than avoiding their questions

I started to practice them. I over-researched so that I knew that there was no way they could trip me up. When the questions came . . . I was prepared.

WHEN YOUR NEMESIS BECOMES YOUR QUARRY

Most important, my brain took on a kind of Pit Bullish–Clint Eastwood attitude as my subconscious would silently say, "There you are . . . go ahead . . . make my day!" Because in my mind there was a barrage of knowledge and insights that I was prepared to bring to bear if needed. Because I had drilled it so many times, those gray-haired, dark-spectacled faces had lost most of their emotional charge. I could think clearly because I was emotionally prepared.

A final note on handling objections: Many years ago I went through a very painful divorce. There were many reasons for this, but the major one was that neither of us in the marriage had a stomach for handling conflict. Whenever a conflict arose, we would ignore it, sweep it under the rug or stick it in the closet. We were always cautious of making sure everything was "nice" all the time. The problem was that after enough real conflict got ignored or deferred, it came roaring back with the force of an avalanche, which no one could stop. By avoiding rejection, I ultimately had to deal with it in proportions that were inhuman.

My training in handling objections and rejections and in learning how to prevent going into an emotional meltdown gave me more confidence to handle conflict. I am not saying that I do not get emotional about it. I still suffer the occasional meltdown.

But I can now be objective about it and recover very quickly. Way more than the money it has put in my pocket, it has given me the richest set of relationships with some of the most powerful and dynamic people in the world. Most important, it has given me the relationship of my dreams with my wife, Eileen. If you learn nothing else from this book, learn this one!

14

Guard Dogs and Pigs

Many pedigree SalesDogs are sometimes intimidated by the ferocious "guard dog." Ferocious and protective of their master's time and energy, these dogs are the ones in charge of "screening" their master's calls—the gatekeeper.

There has been more written about how to outsmart the gatekeeper than probably anything else in sales—hundreds of tricky techniques and smart lines to find clever ways of getting around these personalities to the "decision-maker."

The problem is, most of these fiercely defensive and protective Rottweilers and Dobermans have heard every trick under the sun and are much too smart to fall for any of them.

No dog in his or her right mind is going to try to take on a 125-pound German Shepherd at the front gate. You could throw him a steak laced with sleeping tablets, but wouldn't it just be easier to make friends?

The more you push the stronger they will get. So take a leaf out of a Mel Gibson movie. In *Lethal Weapon 3* Mel was suddenly confronted in a narrow corridor by a snarling Rott-weiler. Faced with the prospect of being dinner, he opted for the most successful sales approach yet. He got down on the floor, rolled his big eyes and started whining and whimpering like a puppy. After a few seconds, instead of his being ripped to shreds, the attacker was his best buddy, lapping his face and nuzzling his neck.

Whether that would work with a real Rottweiler, I don't know, and I'm not really prepared to test the theory! But the concept is sound. Make the guard dogs your friends. Better to have that mound of muscle and tenacity on your side than to have them fighting you. Go to their level; talk to them in ways that they can understand.

The standard question they ask is, "I take X's calls. What is this all about?" Rather than give them some stock line to get around them, say, "Great! Let me tell you about the product," or, "Let me tell you about what I would like to find out about your company." Be friendly, humble and approachable—NEV-ER patronize the gatekeepers.

Treat them as though they were the decision-maker. So of-ten in sales training we are told, "Don't waste time with any-one but the decision-maker." Sometimes that is rubbish, because it may be that at this moment the personal assistant is the decision-maker—he or she is deciding whether you are even going to make it in the front door. Treat him or her with respect and honesty and very soon you will probably hear something like, "You know, you really need to talk to so-and-so about this because they would know more than me."

If you do this well, you will have built an internal ally and referral. Make him or her a friend by filling him or her in on it. It is never a waste of time to build rapport, and it can often pay off later.

Bone: I have learned in corporate sales to "honor thy client's secretary." Remember their names and their needs and remember to thank them whenever you can. They can be your biggest ally or your biggest nightmare.

And then there are the PIGS.

As a puppy, a dog will retrieve anything that you throw. As they get older they become more discerning about what they are going to muddy their paws over. The same is true of SalesDogs.

The ability to determine whether the prospect is a simple "looker," a "first-timer" or a bona-fide prospect will come with experience. In my career and in my conversations with all the great salespeople out there, no one is excluded from the hunt. You never know what the hot buttons are until you ask. In the beginning, spending a lot of time learning how to qualify a lead is a waste of time. Plus it nullifies the valuable one-to-one learning experiences that must be had along the way.

However, there is one animal that all dogs with experience should learn to avoid—the PIG! Of all the barnyard animals, the pig is actually considered one of the brightest animals, although that has done nothing to improve its hygiene or sense of humor! The thing about pigs is that, in addition to being very smart, they are also very "pig-headed."

When I was a kid, we had two German Shepherds on our dairy farm. They would hang out, chase or play with every animal on the farm except the pigs. The pigs were the only animals that would not play: All they would do was grunt and waddle around. If the dogs really tried to get them to play, the pigs would ultimately get so annoyed they would suddenly turn and attack. Ever seen a prospect or a person like that?

There's wisdom in an old expression that my grandfather told me and that my friends and I have bantered around for many years in sales and in teaching. You may have heard the saying "Don't try to teach a pig to sing because it annoys the pig and it can't carry a tune anyway."

Pigs are the people that, in the face of indisputable reason, logic and personal advantage, choose instead to snort, grunt, argue and be belligerent. They don't want to listen and they certainly don't want to buy. They only want to wallow in their mud pit and they want you to get in with them so that they can feel justified in their own negative mess.

There is a saying that the customer is always right. I would qualify that by saying that the RIGHT customer is always right. In other words, there are some people out there who, no matter what you do or say or offer, are going to be pigs. They do not want to cooperate, they do not want to agree and they definitely do not want to sing your song! All they want to do is challenge you and confront you and string you along. Don't waste your time. Heaven knows how much time in my life was spent trying to convince a pig of something when it probably would have preferred to be left alone.

There are some people that should be left alone. Good SalesDogs recognizes a "pig" when they see one. My friend Robert Kiyosaki is fond of saying, "If you spend time arguing with an idiot, you now have two idiots!"

DON'T TRY TO TEACH PIGS HOW TO SING

The Hunt!

THE "DOG DOO-DOO-SIMPLE" SALESDOG CYCLE

Whether you are a Retriever, Pit Bull, Poodle, Chihuahua, Basset Hound or combination of a few of these petulant pooches, every dog must follow the same formula for sales success. The variation lies only in the style and approach of the execution of that formula.

In all my years in sales and in all my years in working with great salespeople, I have found that the sales process is fundamentally very simple. In this book I have attempted to dispel some of the myths around selling and give you the insights and insider secrets that took me years to discover. No one wants to share this information, because it is usually hard-won with blood, sweat and a tidal wave of tears!

I have given you the critical mindsets and shortcut techniques to raise your effectiveness and find the pot of gold you seek. Don't waste too much of your time on the other stuff. If your mind is right, the rest will follow.

Have you ever seen a Terrier tied to a lamppost for two

minutes while his owner steps into the local 7-Eleven to purchase a lottery ticket? He will tie himself up in knots until he has almost cut off the circulation in his little overactive legs.

That's exactly what we as SalesDogs do with every surefire selling theory, strategy and system to emerge into an excited and expectant market.

There is nothing sophisticated about direct sales. It all comes down to three basic parts:

- Prospects
- Appointments—either telephone or face-to-face
- Making arrangements (closing)

Gaining Prospects

This is just a game, a simple and fun game. It is not a measure of your self-worth or intelligence.

A dog with a ball will hit on every person in the park until someone agrees to throw it for him or her. They know that eventually some kind soul out there will throw it, that it's not a matter of if but when. As a SalesDog you have to have the same attitude.

Major bone: *Sales is a pure energy business*. When two people come together in a sales situation, the person with the highest energy wins!

HIGHEST ENERGY WINS

TO QUALIFY OR NOT TO QUALIFY, THAT IS THE QUESTION

There has been a lot said about whether you should spend time qualifying your leads. Is it valuable to spend the time to find out if they might be interested in your product or service versus just asking everyone? I do not believe you should worry about qualifying prospects in the beginning, for four reasons:

1. Sales is an energy business—what you expend comes back. So just getting out there and speaking to people is valuable from an energy-generation point of view.

2. You could be wrong. You might think prospect X has no obvious use for your product but you don't know that for sure and you don't know what he or she knows. It may be that he or she has a friend that is just desperate for your exact product and can't find it anywhere. You would never know that.

3. It will assist you to get desensitized to rejection, and you get to practice your objections on a relatively unimportant prospect.

4. The time you waste trying to work out if someone is interested could be more effectively used by just asking him or her!

Your motto needs to be "Yes!" Say "Yes" to everything. Yes, you will go to the party. Yes, you will call someone's friend. Yes, you will volunteer to help a colleague or friend. All you want to do is get in contact with anyone who might have the remotest interest. You do not care if they like you, hate you, have money or no money. Just get in front of them. Leads are everywhere. A phone call, a friend of a friend, a random calling to a page in the phone book, a phone barrage—it doesn't matter.

STEP ONE

You should never be talking to anybody who does not know who you are.
Certainly you should never talk to anyone who doesn't know
who you are until you have talked to everyone who does! You
should be seeing people who were referred to you or who have
answered your marketing materials.

Remember that all marketing materials—mail, fax, adver-
tisements or web pages—must include an offer that compels a
person to respond and ask for more information. It could be a
line on your home page that offers a free report for signing up.
How about an offer in a sales letter that offers a free consultation valued at $250 if taken advantage of by the end of the
month? Use your imagination.

Gaining prospects is the art of gaining interest through
connections. There is always somebody who knows somebody. Look in annual reports, trade journals, business directo-
ries, news articles and periodicals for names to send inquiries
to. Prospects can be bought on lists, from other companies
and from sources that see benefits to you offering your product or opportunity to their customers. I have often paid a royalty to others for the use of their databases if any of their
customers result in a sale. If you are Pit Bull, you can go out
and cold-call to your heart's content. For myself, I learned
from the Poodle that prospecting is all about connections.
Who do you know that knows lots of people? Ask them about
who they think would be interested in your product, service
or opportunity. Talk to past users, customers, friends, and ask
anyone and everyone for a lead. That will begin the ball
rolling. It's a simple process: get a source or multiple sources
of leads, send them an offer and see who puts up their hand
for more info. There are your prospects. The rest should all be
by referral.

STEP TWO

Make initial contact in whatever way you are most comfortable. Each breed leans toward a particular method of communication. The Pit Bull likes the phone and has little patience for anything else. The Retriever and the Basset prefer an introductory letter, because it is less confrontational and less imposing. The Chihuahua likes the speed and technology of e-mail and the Poodle prefers face-to-face because he can dazzle with his presence, but if it's not possible then a well-produced brochure and well-crafted sales letter is the order of the day—it's all about image and first impression.

Most one-to-one sales begin with a phone call. If you have Pit Bull tendencies, cold-calling doesn't faze you, but for the rest of the kennel the phone call is probably the second line of communication after some initial introduction, piece of marketing material or referral. After one of these initial contacts, then call prospects and either:

1. Thank them for their time, assure them you won't take up much of their time, and introduce yourself and your product or service.
2. Thank them for their time, assure them you won't take up much of their time, and ask if they received the introductory communication you sent and whether they have any questions.
3. Thank them for their time, assure them you won't take up much of their time, and offer to provide more information, clarification or specifics regarding the product or service.

Remember to always be polite and enthusiastic, and don't talk too much. Ask them when would be a good time to meet with them and set an appointment. If they don't have a time in mind, suggest one or several. Your goal in this phone call is simply to get an appointment to meet with them.

If your sales are done over the telephone, then ask if this would be an appropriate time or if another time would be more suitable—and set that up. Always try to get prospects to give you permission to contact them again within a specific period of time, thereby getting permission to keep the lines of communication open between you.

After the initial telephone call, construct a simple, very short, one-paragraph letter thanking prospects for taking the time to speak with you and telling them that you are looking forward to meeting with them at the specified time and place. Tell them to feel free to call you any time they have any questions. But most of all, sincerely thank them for their interest and their time. (You should make a habit of sending thank-you notes after every interaction.) If cost is an issue, or you have thousands of prospects, then thank-you letters can be e-mailed to keep costs down.

STEP THREE

If you haven't done so already, do your market research now. Learn everything you can about prospects, their business, their industry or how they received the information originally. Being equipped with information will give you confidence and show prospects that you take them seriously and have taken time to find out *their* needs.

Prepare a list of questions that you would like to ask the prospect in advance, and rehearse them if you've never done this before. Rehearse this with a colleague, who may even ask you some questions or offer some objections so that you can get some practice in fielding these types of questions. That way you will not be surprised or flustered when the prospect asks simple questions.

It is also very important to know to whom you are talking. Quickly determine what kind of person you are talking to. Most salespeople forget this and it can be fatal. If you talk to the prospect in your terms and from your perspective, you could very easily never truly connect with each other and wonder why!

Each prospect is also a breed who has particular calling cards that you should know and look out for. Once you recognize the breed, communicate in the prospect's style—so you are both speaking the same language.

If the prospect is a:

Pit Bull:

- He may be controlling, abrupt and bottom-line-oriented, so make your comments quick and to the point.
- He may not need lots of socializing.
- Proposals should be brief.
- Relate things in terms of immediate bottom-line benefits to him.
- Do not beat around the bush.
- Ask for his opinions about next steps.
- Highlight key events to take place.
- Go light on the detail.

Chihuahua:

- He is detail- and research-oriented.
- Provide all of the backup material, including facts and figures.
- Accuracy is critical for Chihuahuas, so triple-check everything (no typos!).
- Require good and solid proof.

- Make a detailed proposal.
- Provide testimonials from credible sources.
- Speak clearly and back everything up with facts.
- He will want to see a plan.

Poodle:

- He is image conscious, socially adept, loves to talk, knows the market trends.
- Be sure to personally connect.
- Use referrals.
- List benefits to him in terms of image.
- Is there someone else he was to answer to?
- Being first on the block may be important (seen as an innovator).
- Compliment him on things he has done.
- Ask his opinions.

Retriever:

- He is service-conscious and friendly.
- Focus on after-sales support.
- Follow-through is critical.
- Be friendly, connect personally, ask about him personally.
- Talk in terms of long-term futures.
- Work begins after the sale.
- Offer to do whatever you can for him.
- Ask for referrals.
- He will want to see a plan.

Basset Hound:

- He is very one-to-one, value-oriented and seeks a personal connection.
- Ask for his needs.

- Stress loyalty, service, credibility and value.
- Spend time with him.
- Be on his side.
- Sympathize with his situation.
- Practice humility.

While prospects are talking it is important to begin to watch them physically, mentally and emotionally. Model their body language subtly. In other words, if their arms are crossed, cross your arms. If their legs are crossed, cross your legs. If they are leaning forward, lean forward with them. Do not be too dramatic about this. This is done simply in order for you to subconsciously begin to build rapport with the person you're talking to.

If they talk quickly with lots of hand movements, they are probably very visual. Therefore when you speak to them you should speak to them in terms of pictures, visions, painting a picture for them. Ask them if they can *see* what you are talking about.

If they talk in slow, soothing tones and seem to think before they speak, they are probably very kinesthetic (feeling-oriented). When you talk to these people you must also speak slowly, in more soothing tones. More important, talk to them in terms of how the project *feels*. Ask them if they can get a *sense* of what you're talking about. Ask them to trust their feelings or intuition about which way they feel they should go. These indicators will help communicate more clearly to this type of person what it is you're trying to say.

There is a third category of prospect, which is what we call auditory. These prospects seem to talk in a sing-song fashion. The deal would have to "*sound* good to them." With these people, who are a minority, you want to use words like "listen," "hear," "ring," "sound good to you?"

The reason for these actions is that they will build a subconscious or unconscious rapport between you and the person to whom you are talking. As a matter of fact, if you're only speaking to him on the phone, it is probably good to have the conversation while standing up and walking around, preferably with a headset. This gives more energy to what you have to say, and the chances are that the other person will feel that energy as well. It allows you to think more clearly and also to be able to speak in visual terms or kinesthetic terms even though you may not have direct eye contact with the person that you are talking to. You might even consider putting a mirror up at your desk so that you can look at yourself periodically in any given phone conversation. If your facial expression is contorted and tense, I can guarantee you that will also be the energy that you are conveying across the telephone.

When we were in the trucking business, we had to deal with a lot of customer service, especially with people who were not always very pleased. As we were a time-sensitive delivery business, there were many opportunities for service failures. All of our customer-service people had mirrors in front of their desks to remind them to attempt to keep their energy high and smiles big. You could tell if a truck was late making a delivery because you would see at least three or four people with headsets on pacing around their desks looking at the mirror continually to keep themselves from getting depressed, defensive or frustrated. It works wonders.

FINAL WORD ON GAINING PROSPECTS

At the prospect stage, the important thing is action and energy. The higher the energy, the greater the results—use the mindset techniques discussed in earlier chapters to keep your energy high at all times.

It's a funny thing: Once you start to follow up, you get so busy following up that it creates an energy field of its own. All of a sudden people will start seeking you out to ask questions, calling you, wanting to know what you know, wanting to talk to you, wanting to "toss the ball" with you.

When you direct a team of salespeople all you have to do is keep them fed and nourished. Just get them to call and market like wild SalesDogs and not to worry about anything else, and that includes sales.

That pivotal day when I made the sixty-eight cold calls was a classic example. It was a game. I was not trying to sell anything. I was just being a SalesDog. Out of that barrage I sold nothing and only got one appointment, but the next day I got one sale and three appointments on six calls! It's an energy thing.

Running from office to office may sound a bit Pit Bullish, and it is a little. It is more about putting out energy. You may try it and find it uncomfortable. That's OK. Use whatever you are most comfortable with to talk to and communicate with as many people as possible. It's not about running through doors to accost office managers, but about putting out the energy. Do it through marketing, do it through servicing, do it through making friends, do it through data dumping—but just do it! With the creation of the energy, you have two goals: lots of people and lots of appointments.

Appointments

Once you have whipped up the energy surrounding your prospects, appointments or permission to call again is sure to follow. This is a critical step in establishing your relationship with them. Here are the steps to follow to ensure that your appointments ultimately lead to sales.

STEP FOUR

On the day of the appointment or scheduled phone call be sure that you are prepared in the following way:

- Be well-groomed and well-dressed. Even if all your sales are done on the phone, if you look good, you feel good and that comes across in your communication. Being dressed professionally shifts your mind into success mode and you will lift your game. Remember that first impressions take a matter of seconds. Some people dig themselves a hole before they even step out of the door. My friend Sherry Maysonave, in her book *Casual Power,* states that the percentage difference in sales volume between those who groom and dress properly and those who do not is astronomical. As a rule, always attempt to dress one level above your prospect. Never make sales calls while looking too casual.
- Do whatever is necessary to set your emotions and thoughts in the right place. In other words, choose the emotion that you want before the appointment. Be excited, be enthusiastic, and be happy. If you do this, the outcome of your appointment will reflect that mindset.
- Be on time and arrive at your destination at least five minutes before the meeting time. If the appointment was set over a week previously, call in advance to confirm the appointment before you get in your car. This shows courtesy and good planning.

Remember that if you have agreed to call back on a specific date—make sure you call. Many of us seem to think that a telephone appointment is less important than a face-to-face appointment. However, if you do not do what you say you will do this early in the relationship, what faith should this sales prospect have that you will behave any differently if you do business together?

Do what you say you will do, when you said you would do it. It is very important to keep your agree-

DARLA'S WARDROBE
WAS QUESTIONABLE

ments. And if anything does change, inform the other person as soon as possible.

STEP FIVE

As you walk into the appointment, or make that telephone call, remember to focus on what you want to happen as an outcome to the meeting. Before the meeting, attempt to remember a similar positive experience from your past where everything went really well. Anchor that positive moment by reliving the moment in your head and allowing yourself to feel that emotion.

As you meet the prospect face-to-face for the first time, be sure to smile and offer your hand in handshake—if that's customary in your region. (As a note on handshakes . . . don't crush the hand and don't wimp out. Meet and match the firmness of the prospect's grip. If mishandled, this can set up a momentary feeling of discomfort, which is not the way to begin a relationship.) Wait to be directed to a seat by the prospect before sitting.

If you are making a telephone call, it is even more important that you smile, as this will come across in your communication.

Design a conversation solely to find out as much as you can about the prospect: about what they do, why they do it, why they like it, what their ideals are and what their frustrations and problems are. DO NOT TRY TO SELL. Spend the time asking relevant questions. DO NOT allow yourself to pitch even if they ask. You cannot pitch till you fill the bucket with the bits and pieces of data about them. Have fun. Be truly INTERESTED and do not try to be INTERESTING—yet! If you have to talk about you, talk about your experiences related to the product or service, preferably in your own life. Do not pitch!

The great SalesDogs are eternal students of human psychology, body language, mirroring and matching and anything else that will help them build rapport. The SalesDogs rapport-building kit takes minutes to review and yields instant connection, understanding and affinity from nearly any customer you talk to either in person, on the phone or across the Internet.

Ask the questions and LISTEN to the answers. Early questions can be questions such as:

- How did you hear about our service or product?
- What particular needs do you have regarding our service or product?
- When this product or service was referred to you, what was it that specifically sparked your interest?

Listen to obtain and remember important information, and you should also physically show prospects that you are listening intensely. This will let them know that you are truly interested and totally into what they're thinking. As they speak, be careful not to interrupt, no matter how excited you get about something they just said. Many times salespeople will jump into the middle of the prospect's dissertation with a solution or a great idea that they are convinced the prospect would be interested in, based upon what he just said. Do not make this mistake. Listen all the way through. You may be excited about something but remember, all the prospect wants is to tell you what's on his mind. He is not interested in what *you* have to say until he has finished what *he* has to say, so keep quiet and listen.

Continue to ask open questions (ones that can't be answered with a one-word answer), such as why, when, how many. The second level of questions that you ask should be questions regarding the prospects themselves, their business, the nature of their needs and what they specifically want, if they have not already told you. In other words, take the time now to find out more about their business, if this is a business sale. If this is a retail sale try to find out more about what they would be using the product or service for. Learn as much as you possibly can.

If this is a network marketing sale, find out what their particular goals are for getting involved or even being interested in this type of business opportunity. Listen closely and find out these three things:

1. Their specific tangible goals
2. Their opinion about how to implement or make use of the product or service
3. Their emotional expectation

What you want to find out is how they want to feel, or how they would feel if in fact this product or service fulfilled all their expectations. This is important, because when you begin to give them answers, you must deliver on all three of these criteria.

If prospects simply want you to tell them about your product or service or opportunity, and insist that you go first, you should politely agree to do that after a couple of very quick questions. It is important to be sure that you are able to listen first for several reasons. It gives you time to relax. It allows you to understand the important things about the prospect—their energy, their emotions, their needs, their expectations, their body language and many other things as well.

STEP SIX

The only outcome of this first contact should be to set up another time to present a proposal, a draft solution or a process by which customers can reach the goals that they mentioned to you. If you can do this in the first conversation that's great. However, do not be frustrated if you don't close the deal on the first call. Remember, this is about building a relationship.

Your goal is actually twofold in this first encounter. The first goal, as I mentioned, is to create an opportunity or another appointment or another time to come back with more detailed answers to their questions. Your second goal is to make an agreement with them for no other purpose than to simply prove that you can keep an agreement. (Of course you don't tell prospects this.) You make a simple agreement such as, "I will call you the day after tomorrow to let you know about my progress," or "I will send some brochures, more testimonials or referrals your way within the next forty-eight hours." Even if prospects do not want these things, it is important for you to create an opportunity to make an agreement and to keep it. This begins to set a track record, to establish unconsciously in their minds that you are dependable and that you do what you say. For each subsequent conversation that you have with prospects there is only one goal. At the very least, ensure you have another agreement so that you can fulfill it some time in the very near future.

Remember, good dogs always bring the ball back once it is thrown. They bring it back again and again and again and again. YOU have to create a ball for them to throw by making an agreement to service them somehow. Once you give them the ball, you actually are throwing it for them, and then you begin retrieving. By doing this, you plant a subconscious message of trustworthiness and care in their minds. You establish a track record of trust in their minds so later when it comes time to decide between you and someone else, they remember that you are a SalesDog who does what he says he will.

Subsequent appointments are designed to present more materials, give and present proposals, "make arrangements" and sign orders.

Consider, for example, the story of Francine. Francine was an extremely personable and caring person. Her sincerity was rivaled only by her intelligence and genuine interest in others.

Every time Francine came back to the office after a sales call, her manager would ask, "How many did you close today?" It drove her nuts. Especially when she could not give him the response that he wanted. She grew very frustrated with her job and subsequently left. She vowed that sales was not for her and that she would simply go do something else that was less stressful and with more steady income. A friend of hers recommended that she go to an interview for a sales position, marketing Internet services by telephone. She groaned that there was no way she was going back to the pressure of sales—especially phone sales. Yet she had the time, so she went. She loved the services and built instant rapport with the manager, Emma, who was doing the interviewing. She voiced her concern and reluctance to the manager in the interview. Emma encouraged Francine to give it another try. She told Francine that her only goal with each call was to set up another opportunity to call the prospect to either give them additional information, follow up on a commitment that she made or check on status. Emma knew that Francine was a true Retriever, willing to serve, and a Basset Hound with the ability to win anyone's heart. Even though her conversations were via phone, Francine became the number-one Sales-Dog of the team. She never worried about "closing" again. All she did was try for the next phone appointment, set the date and, like clockwork, follow up. For Francine, every call was a chance to serve. Every phone appointment was designed to build a deeper and deeper relationship until it was simply time to deliver.

STEP SEVEN

My favorite thing to do when selling has gotten me in a bit of trouble over the years but has kept me number one for the past twenty-plus years, and it has kept tons of cash rolling through the door. My tech assistants hated me for it and my business partners spent many sleepless nights covering me for it, and to this day it sometimes keeps me up at night, but I do it nonetheless.

YOU GIVE THEM WHATEVER THEY WANT!

Yep, that's it. It is what I call the "magic wand" approach. "If I could wave a magic wand to create the ideal solution, provide the ideal service, the best policy, the perfect house, what would it be?" I listen, ask a few more specific questions and prepare to deliver. I will go to the ends of the planet to find that ball for them no matter where it is thrown. I will keep them apprised of the search, of the creation, of the trials and tribulations along the way (remember reasons to stay in contact) and somehow find a way to solve the problems they have.

Typical examples of demands that customers might make when you give them the magic wand question: "I want a training program that will change the attitude of my managers to that of being coaches instead of dictators." "I need my cargo delivered in New York every Monday before 9:00 A.M." "I need a software system that will eliminate the repetition of dual posting of payroll taxes." "I want a way to achieve financial freedom without quitting my normal job."

These days I actually use this technique and pump up the stakes even higher by guaranteeing that if I do not deliver what they want, they do not have to pay me. I have only once given someone his money back, and only because I was not satisfied with the result of the training.

You see, for most reasonable requests, there IS a solution. A great SalesDog can find it. A friend of mine was searching for an investment advisor and a new accountant. He interviewed many quality prospects but was never satisfied. He was at a party and happened to explain his plight to a young fellow who happened to be an accountant. Wisely he asked my friend the question. "If I could wave a magic wand, what is it that you really want in terms of investment strategies?" My friend was a little miffed because up to then he had only been told what he could NOT do. After a moment he answered, "Well, I would like to be able to invest on a tax-deferred basis and ultimately withdraw the money at some future date tax-free." The young fellow chuckled and said, "Wouldn't everyone like that?" He then quickly added that he was not sure what could be done but asked my friend if he would be willing to meet with him, an insurance colleague, a portfolio manager and a tax attorney in his office sometime the following week. My friend was ecstatic. I do not know if he got his entire wish, but when I asked him he simply gave me a big grin and said, "I have a team that handles it." In that case a wise accountant, who was unafraid to sniff out solutions that he did not have in his own bag of tricks, obtained a lifelong customer for himself and several associates.

In the IT business, my tech assistants would scream at me and tell me that our computers could not do what I told the customer they could do. I told them that we would have to figure out how to do it. We usually found a way to do it, or were able to find another system that could do it for them. I lost a few sales that way, but very few, and certainly those that were lost became huge burdens on my competitors because of the heightened expectations of the prospect.

Making Arrangements (Closing)

STEP EIGHT

Whether in the initial call or a subsequent call, there will come a time when it is your turn to deliver information. After you've asked the questions and feel fairly comfortable with who the person is and feel that the relationship has begun to build a bit, begin to answer his questions in terms of how your product or service or opportunity will solve his problems physically, mentally and emotionally. Notice his reaction. Notice his body-language responses to the things that you say. Nodding? Crossing his arms with furrowed brow? Doing other work while you are talking? Looking at his watch? Eyes staring off into space?

Take notice of all these physical cues and respond to them as quickly as you can. Do not make the mistake of going on and on when the body language of the prospect clearly tells you that he is **not interested** or that he does not agree. If the prospect begins to do other work while you're talking, that is not a good sign. You must stop at that point and check in with the prospect. If you are getting negative body language or sense things slipping away, stop and ask the customer or prospect if he understands. How does he feel? Does he understand what he has heard? Ask any question that will elicit a response so that you can know how you are doing. Do not keep digging a hole if you're not sure if this call is going properly. Ask questions. If his body language or responses are favorable, that is a good thing. Check in with him again periodically and ask how he's dealing with this information. Be flexible. Change course or direction on a moment's notice if you need to. Do not be Silly Putty, but do follow the lead of the prospect.

When it is time, begin to ask him his views of how this product, service or opportunity will be implemented. Begin to get him to speak in terms of how he would like to see the process evolve. When is it time to do this? It is time to do this WHENEVER you have a sense that the prospect understands, agrees or is in line with what you are talking to him about. If you have handled most of his major objections, and if you have provided satisfactory answers to the questions that he has offered, and if there seem to be no more issues on the table, that is the time to begin to ask those questions.

I call this part of the process "making arrangements." **You should eliminate the word "closing" from your sales vocabulary. Nobody likes to be closed in. And many salespeople are afraid of closing.** Just take the perspective that **you're going to begin making arrangements** for installation, implementation, delivery or enrollment. First, ask how he sees it. Or has a sense of it. Once the prospect begins to think in those terms it becomes simply a matter of asking him "when," "where" and "how." When would you like to take delivery? How quickly would you like to begin? How soon would you like to begin to take advantage of this opportunity?

Along the way, and probably before this arrangement

stage, there will undoubtedly be questions and possible objections. Remember to drill objections in advance. As fast as you can, as many as you can and as often as you can. The reason for this is so that objections become simply part of the conversation and not some traumatic emotional experience. Answer all objections and questions as clearly and as briefly as you can. However, it is appropriate in most cases to answer a question or an objection with an initial question, such as, "Thank you, I understand that you feel this may be a little bit over budget. Why do you say that?" Or, "You mentioned that the timing is not good for you right now. Why would that be the case?"

By asking questions to truly find out "why" instead of trying to trap the prospect, you show genuine interest in his plight. Be sure to continuously relate the real, tangible, emotional, and irresistible benefits of having what you are offering. Never ever try to manipulate prospects. They will sense it and like a trapped animal will fight to be released. Sales is about making friends and relationships. It is not about winning the battle of wits.

That is why you do not have to be an attack dog to make a lot of money in sales. Pit Bulls, Poodles, Retrievers, Chihuahuas, or Basset Hounds can do this process equally well with their own styles.

The intensity of the Chihuahua will build tremendous rapport because the prospect will perceive true interest and concern. The true Retriever will offer the support and understanding that is unique to its breed and will warm the prospect from that perspective. The Poodle will offer its professional view of the solution in such a way as to make the prospect feel confident in the strength and the validity of the service, product or opportunity. The Basset Hound is a master at building rapport. His natural listening capability and sympathetic understanding of the customer's plight will endear him to the prospect for months to come. Big Dogs live for this moment, and the more that there is on the line the happier they are. Pit Bulls have to be careful to be patient, to turn objections into further conversation, and to at least pretend that they are interested. Hints to Pit Bulls: Stay in present time! Do not over-think or try to second-guess yourself or the prospect.

This cycle could be one appointment or it could be six. Use your judgment about when the energy is beginning to dwindle. Attempt to end the conversation before the energy gets too low. You want to begin with medium energy and end with high energy. Leave on an expectation of more and better information, which you will provide. In each conversation always ask them "making-arrangements questions," subtly at first, and in more detail later, as most objections and questions have been answered.

Most prospects who are genuinely interested will be very clear about the arrangements they want to make with you. Some, however, will not be interested. That's OK. Do not take it personally. Do you buy everything that you see in a store all the time? Of course not. You may not have what this person really has in mind. That's OK. Feel free to admit it as soon as you perceive that you do not have the proper solution for this customer. That will build tremendous credibility. If you have to bow out of the deal, and you have done so honorably, then feel free to ask the prospect, based upon what you have told him so far, if he would happen to know of anyone else who might be interested in this product, service or opportunity. Ask him for the name and number and whether he would be willing to give this new prospect a call in advance to tell him you will be calling on him.

There are others who get cold feet. Everything has been answered and the prospect really does want the product or service but cannot seem to make a decision. This can be very frustrating for a salesperson who has put in a lot of work and energy up to this point. Be careful! Do not get impatient! If you try to pull the trigger too fast here, you could blow the whole thing. If you are faced with this dilemma, you might try this. Instead of asking the "arrangement" questions again, simply *tell* the prospect when, where or how you will deliver. Notice his response. He may simply agree and go along with you, and then the deal is done. If he still hesitates, you can be a little bit Pit Bullish. A response that has worked for me has been a statement like, "OK, it is up to you. Let me know what you want me to do to make this happen for you. I am happy to do whatever you would like me to do at this point. Is there one thing that needs to take place before we can begin this process?"

Remember, if you have been a good Retriever up till now, making arrangements will not be difficult. Ask the prospect if he can envision himself in the future with this product, service or opportunity—what it would be like. Once he talks about it, then you can simply ask if it is OK to get started now.

I would love to say that going through this cycle one time will guarantee you sales. That is not true. The steps can be a repetitive loop in which you continue to cycle with a customer. Selling is like dancing. You move and sway and bow and twirl. The difference in sales is that the music never really stops. You can always come back and dance with that same partner again later if you need to.

Be sure to always tell prospects about the services and support that you will be providing for them *after the sale*. Tell them that the sale is the beginning, not the end. Once the sale is made, the real work begins in terms of support, installation, application and success. It is very powerful to be able to *guar-*

antee that if that does not happen you will be happy to refund their entire investment without question. This takes all of the risk away from the customer and rests it with you.

Never be afraid to ask, "How soon can we begin?" If you ask the same way every time, the customer will feel pressured, so ask in several different ways and at several different times.

If your product requires a longer sales cycle, your job with each interaction with the customer is to first make an agreement and keep it and also to get him to commit to some further action. This could be the completion of financing forms. It could be completing a survey. It could be visiting a user's site. It could be talking to a current user.

Remember that there is a point in time when the buyer considers the sale to be consummated. There will be a moment of euphoria in his mind, a time when he is proud of his innovative decision or a time when he can actually visualize the benefits of what he is buying. That is the time to strike with the perfect question. "Do you know anyone else who might be interested?" This could be some time before signing an order or days or weeks after the deal is done, but almost *never* when the prospect is actually signing or concluding the sale. Regardless of what appears to be his frame of mind, there is always a point of fear, of indecision and possible second-guessing that happens at the moment of sale. Don't jam his space!

Do not ask this question until he is in that settled and proud state of mind or you could give him buyer's remorse, the feeling that you are just interested in making the sale and not about the relationship. Time that question right, though, and he will absolutely give you names. You will be on a roll and you will never have to call anyone unannounced again!

In a Nutshell

GAINING PROSPECTS

1. Speak to people you know first.
2. Make initial contact the way you are most comfortable.
3. Do your market research.

APPOINTMENTS

4. Make a great first impression.
5. Focus on what you want to happen at the appointment in advance, not on your fears.
6. Make an appointment to call or visit again—a reason to stay in touch.
7. Give them whatever they want.

MAKING ARRANGEMENTS (CLOSING)

8. Ask questions and handle objections. Listen and watch your prospect for buying signals. "Make arrangements" to close the deal in a manner suitable to the client—not you.

Bone: "Closing" is an attitude—not something that happens at the end of a call. You should *always* be asking, arranging, and trying to implement and solve as soon as possible.

16

Whose Fire Hydrant Is This Anyway?

SECRETS OF TERRITORY MANAGEMENT

There is no dog in the world that is not intimately aware of its own territory and when it has been intruded upon. While your playful pooch will cock his leg with what seems like indiscriminate abandon to mark its territory, most, but not all, Sales-Dogs have a more civilized means of marking their domain.

Territories for SalesDogs can be geographic, by product line, by line of business, by target market group or by network. Regardless of how the lines are drawn, the rules for how to mark and protect your territory remain the same.

A good SalesDog must learn to stake out the boundaries of his or her territory. While it is not socially acceptable to "mark" your turf, defining and managing a territory can be done in many ways and accomplishes several important things.

Contrary to popular belief, staking out the territory is *not* done just to ward off competitors or encroachers. In sales, the establishment of territories is important to give a SalesDog a sense of what is his or her arena and to enable all creatures in

TERRITORY MANAGEMENT

the area to know who is the "keeper" of the land. By walking the perimeter of the territory enough times, the SalesDog becomes familiar with every scent, every structure and every undulation of the terrain. He or she knows every creature that inhabits that area, their habits, rituals and customs.

A SalesDog protects its territory, examines it, and is relentlessly curious about every nuance and change that occurs in it. A SalesDog should know in detail about the companies in his or her territory—how they rank in their industries, their management philosophies, whether they are growing or shrinking and on and on. A SalesDog should know just as much about the people he or she has contact with—where they fall in the hierarchy, how they are thought of, which direction their careers are going and the emotional issues that they face. Once this familiarity is formed, all of the creatures begin to look to the SalesDog as the keeper of the land.

I have a friend who has been in the office products business in Sydney for many years. He has enthusiastically and dutifully patrolled that territory ever since he opened up shop. There is not anything that occurs in the office products business in Sydney, or in Australia for that matter, that he doesn't know about. Even though other dogs have occasionally intruded, peed on and scratched through the area, sales continue to flow to him. Those other dogs have all since passed through and he is still there. He has become outrageously successful and the vendor of choice for the largest companies in the region.

Because of his patience and long-term stake in the territory, after a while all of the creatures in that territory turned to him. If you have patience and a long-term view, the cash starts rolling unassisted.

That is why you stake a territory, hold it and work it. Everyone in it should know you, know what you do, and you should be the point of information for anything that breathes a hint of your product or service. Time and territory have taken some of the SalesDogs with the poorest sales techniques and made them very rich.

For young pups this is a hard one, because they're impatient to get results. That is why celebrating and acknowledging small wins along the way is so important for keeping the spirit up over time. Territory management is not difficult: Just keep sniffing and digging around on a regular daily, weekly and monthly basis. It is as important for the prospects to see you digging on a regular basis as it is for you to uncover new and relevant information. Prospects and clients ultimately become attracted to you because you have formed a track record of regularity, dependability and stability in their minds. This is the strength and forte of the Basset Hound, one that other breeds should emulate.

By the way, the technique we discussed earlier about making and keeping agreements with prospects and clients is an essential tool when it comes to territory management. By purposely making the agreement to call, write, stop by, supply with information or provide some business or nonbusiness service, you have systematically formed a track record of trustworthiness in their minds.

While there will always be a new dog on the block to pee on your fire hydrant and scratch at your clients, the wise Sales-Dog continues to be dependable and loyal. You will be seen as a pillar, not a plunderer.

17

Stay Out of the Pound

CAREER PROGRESSION FOR SALESDOGS

One of the reasons that people like you and me are attracted to the high-velocity, high-pressure, high-possibility field of sales is that we love the chase, love the wins and love to do it all over again. We LIVE for the next thrill, the next deal, the next rush, and that type of personality never stops searching. That is a good thing. However, our need for immediate and frequent gratification can lead us astray.

Just like the pooch left at home for too long without company or stimulation, a SalesDog without interaction and results will tear up the house, eat the furniture and wander off, possibly going AWOL.

Great SalesDogs understand the need to focus, commit and be patient. This is true for your industry, your territory and your products. It doesn't make sense to spend time and energy to get to know the territory if, whenever there is a dry patch, you go jumping the fence and jumping ship.

The greatest SalesDogs of all have somehow, over time, developed the discipline of focus and longevity—delayed gratification. Inexperienced SalesDogs, especially some of the more high-strung, perfectionist SalesDogs, have a tendency to panic if sales slow, and even when the sales do arrive they always have one eye on the back door just in case "something better comes up."

The quickest way to find yourself in the pound is to live your life as a SalesDog with a "grass is always greener" mentality. In this business you can go from a Legend to a loser in the space of about five minutes. That's the nature of the game. You are only as good as your last sale.

SalesDogs are driven by the dollar, and that is a powerful motivator for many of us. However, the constant drive for bigger, better, more can mean that we jump ship just as our ship is about to come in. It takes time, effort, care, dedication, service, loyalty and intention to build relationships and foster trust. And too much wandering simply negates all that work and stops the momentum. We all dream of the "order-taker" situation where people seek you out and ask to buy. Often, if you spend your time wandering from company to company, or worse, industry to industry, it is someone else who comes in after you who benefits from your hard work. You will never reap the rewards and get the results if you stray too much.

So what happens to dogs that stray?

Ultimately, they become a nuisance and are sent to the pound. The lucky ones may get a second chance, but most get neutered, spayed, put out to pasture or put down!

There are many wandering SalesDogs that long to sell again the way that they "used to." Even long-wandering Sales-Dogs still cling to that five minutes of fame where they were a Legend. They retell the stories of great past conquests to anyone who will listen.

Yet, for many of these dogs the fighting spirit has been

surgically removed, not by the vet's scalpel, but by the market, which ultimately supports the familiar smiling face of the focused and committed SalesDog and rejects the wandering, whining, flee-infested stray looking for a quick scrap or deal.

The world is littered with thousands of great dogs that could be champions and great hunters with the right training and ownership. The same is true of SalesDogs. One of the problems with early success is that some SalesDogs get impatient for a repeat performance and cannot weather the ebb and flow of the sales energy cycle.

Remember, it's called a sales cycle because it is a cycle. It just keeps going round and round. There will be good and bad, high and low, but every phase will pass.

Frank was one of the hottest network-marketing guys in Toronto. He built one of the fastest-growing networks in a very short time. Impatient for a repeat performance, he jumped to at least six different companies in the space of two years trying to build a similar network. He was on the road to making millions, but he didn't have the staying power or the patience.

Those whom he actually enrolled and who have stayed over the years are all retired now, reaping the benefits of thousands of dollars of passive income each month. The last I heard of him, he was an obscure administrator buried in some large public company, living in the suburbs, still telling others about how great he was in the old days.

My brother is the classic SalesDog. His Basset Houndish approach truly masks a raging Pit Bull underneath. As a young SalesPup he jumped from industry to industry. He went from cargo sales to insurance sales to more insurance sales and ultimately into selling warehousing equipment and warehouse systems. It took years for him to reap the benefits of sales, because try as he might he could not find the right fit. My family was concerned. Would Tim ever make it? Would he be destined to frustration forever?

No way! The wise thing that Tim did was to pick companies along the way that were known across the industry to have the finest training programs available. His transitions were transitions that spanned several years, not several companies in a year. Once he found a product and a service that truly thrilled him (he has always loved playing with trucks and cranes) he was light-years ahead of others competing for the position of Dog Trainer there. His skills and his bank of experience had all built to a peak. He now lives in a big house on several acres of land in one of the nicest areas surrounding Cleveland. I can still remember him saying that even though he was not really pleased with the other positions over the years, he was determined to stay and learn as much as he could before moving on.

You have seen them . . .

The guys who seem to play golf all the time, never have to make cold calls, always get the best referrals and seem to never have to sweat their numbers. They seem to be on a perpetual roll. It is because they have stayed loyal to their owners, their territory and their line of business and over time they have become *the* competition to everyone else. They have earned that enviable position only because they have been there the longest and have the appearance of being the authorities.

The strays that jump from place to place never gain the critical energetic mass that creates the attractive gravity toward them. Ultimately their lack of results generates burnout, creates a negative spiral in their heads that neuters their ability to sell.

I am of the opinion that the profession of sales is the most powerful personal growth endeavor anyone can take on. Why? Because every day when you look in the mirror it forces you to see who you really are. The results you create are a reflection of what you think, what you do, what you feel and even what you avoid.

I have also found that nearly all successful people in the world of business, in every part of the world, can trace their roots back to selling. Their tenacity, their optimism, their resilience are all due to countless encounters with prospects, both large and small.

The first decision is a critical one. Where to go to work?

You see, as a sales professional, you should pick a company based not on the amount of compensation that you will receive initially, but more important, upon the education that you will receive. When choosing a network-marketing company, a real-estate firm, or a corporation, choose it based upon the training that it will provide you.

That will be the best long-term investment you will ever make. Years ago I chose Burroughs (now UNYSIS), but not because of its products. It actually had the most costly and overpriced computer systems in the business at that time, and they were the most difficult to operate. However, their training was vast and extensive. The four years that I spent there not only gave me the tools to sell, but also ingrained the intestinal fortitude to be a real player in the business world.

As a manager, if you are focused on training your pack of dogs, you will win big. If you focus only on the $$$s, your victories will be short and fleeting. As a good SalesDog, you should pick the company that will give you the best training possible. Once you find it, make the commitment to stay there for at least four to five years in order to take advantage of the continual stream of coaching, training and personalized attention that comes with great sales training. The length of time is critical in order to truly build the focus, the skills and the strengths that are necessary. Jumping to new places breaks the flow of training and coaching. The time goes quickly and the financial benefits are enormous if you exercise some persistence and some patience.

That is why I like network-marketing organizations. The good ones offer a tremendous amount of training and mentoring. This is because each person has a vested interest in training the people that he brings in. It puts money directly in his pocket. In this world of e-commerce, e-business and e-learning, networks are everything. Those that invest in training their human resources actually multiply their network's earning power exponentially.

Once you know which breed of dog you are, you need to find a mentor (an alpha dog) who is of different breed, who can give you the skills that you need to be an upper-quadrant Sales-Dog. Pit Bulls need to find mentors who are Poodles or Golden Retrievers in order to add the marketing and service qualities to their repertoire of sales skills. The Basset Hound needs to find a Poodle for marketing and the Poodle needs a bit of the knowledge of the Chihuahua to add some bite to the smooth image.

If a SalesDog stays focused, his career will take a natural progression, like ever-expanding concentric circles. There are five major migrations for the great SalesDog. Each migration is an expanded territory, which presents larger and larger opportunities for reward.

Most young pups begin their sales life by selling some retail product or service for someone else. The job is very sales-oriented and requires very little personal marketing. This could be selling produce, shoes, office supplies or men's clothing in a retail mall. At this stage, the key to success is assertiveness—where you can deal with objections and rejections and close well. You also need high energy and an empathic and attentive nature. This is important for building relationships, follow-up sales, service and problem solving. Work on these skills as a SalesPup and you're headed for an exciting and lucrative career.

CAREER CYCLE

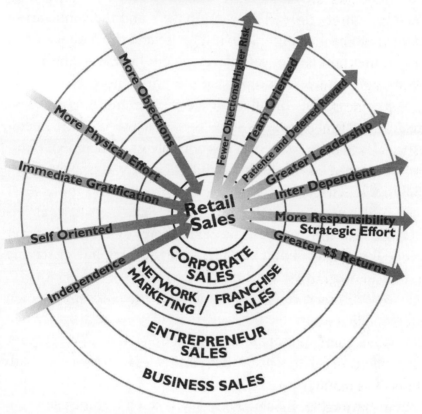

As SalesDogs get bolder and learn more about establishing and maintaining good relationships, they move into corporate sales. They are still selling a product for someone else—such products as business machines, airfreight services or investments—but with higher yields and more complexity in the product and in the relationships.

At this stage you need to hone your face-to-face skills so that you can engender trust. You need to get used to and comfortable with high-level decision-makers and the subtle art of damage control. Being able to improvise and think on your feet is an important part of your development here, as is the ability to simplify complex concepts and present to groups.

These spheres of sales are very safe, and it is in these realms that real SalesDogs show their true breed and temperament. They begin to become comfortable with their own natural talent and the strengths of their breed. At this stage, most SalesDogs can easily generate healthy six-digit incomes.

This is the time NOT TO STRAY! If SalesDogs stray at this stage in their development the next spheres of sales will forever elude them. They simply will not have the discipline or staying power to reap the benefits of Big Dog Dollars.

Within the corporate arena there is the natural transition to managing and directing, yet there may come a time when seasoned SalesDogs catch the scent of much larger prey. The independent streak that drew them into sales may reemerge with passion and intensity.

In phase three, SalesDogs may take on a franchise as an owner or even take on the challenge of building a multilevel organization. They will invest their own time and money, and sell like they have never sold before. The risk is greater, but the rewards can be huge. In fact, there is no ceiling on earnings. It is still a relatively safe sphere because formulas exist for sales and distribution. In this sphere, the SalesDog has protection from some of the dangers of the wild.

To succeed in this sphere, SalesDogs must perfect their ability to speak to groups. They must inspire and be able to transmit emotion, enroll others in their vision and be able to deliver the big picture.

The next sphere for the SalesDog is becoming an entrepreneur and developing his or her own concept, product or service and constructing the infrastructure and business to produce and deliver it. This is done with his own ideas and with his own team. The SalesDog has the job not just of selling to end users, but of enrolling investors, lenders, suppliers and other allies in his vision. A SalesDog's skills must be fine-tuned, because far more than one sale is on the line—other people's money, confidence and support. The failure ratio is very high at this level, but the rewards can be legendary. Just ask Bill Gates or Michael Dell.

Intensity and passion are imperative, because it is often these ingredients that will motivate the team and pull people through the uncertainty. Being able to solve problems creatively combined with an ability to just "find a way" are critical to success in this sphere.

The final sphere for a SalesDog is in not just selling your own product, but actually selling your own business. You move into the realm of being business builder and business seller. There are many happy SalesDogs who went through the swamps and the tangled woodlands to become great business builders. Along the way, their strength and optimism kept them ahead of the aristocratic breeds that jumped into the marketplace without the basics. The underlying strength of each of these individuals is their ability to create a vision and sell others on the vision.

The competitive drive to succeed is here, and the conceptual and strategic abilities to see both the big picture and the detail are a real gift. These SalesDogs are natural marketers and often very systems-oriented. They are rarely one breed—they are more often the best of every single breed: the never-say-die of the Pit Bull; the marketing savvy of the Poodle with the innate understanding that perception equals reality; the data-hungry knowledge bank of the Chihuahua; the underpromise and overdeliver of the Retriever; and the trust and integrity of the Basset. What a pooch!

As you move from one SalesDog sphere of sales to another, the income and opportunities increase exponentially. What is required is more and more personal responsibility for your results, your life and your condition. As you make the transition, the room for blame, easy justifications and shirking of responsibility diminishes. You become accountable for ALL results. This is the part that Basset Hounds understand even as SalesPups and secretly look forward to as they grow up.

In the beginning of the cycle, SalesDogs do more selling, yet as they make the transition to the next level, marketing skills become as important as selling skills. Poodles are good at this and test their marketing skills in lower-risk areas early on.

The risk gets higher, but oddly enough, the rejections and objections get fewer. However, they are more critical, as each rejection can cost a lot in terms of funding strategies, production, support and cash flow.

Most important, the role of the SalesDog changes from the new pup in the pack to the "alpha" dog that lays down the laws of the kennel. More and more leadership is called for as the SalesDog makes the transition to each sphere. Leadership is an automatic by-product for the SalesDog that stays focused and does not stray.

Why is this important?

Because each succeeding sphere puts more and more cash into your pocket. The difference between sphere one and sphere four is easily five to six times greater in terms of cash. The nature of the hunt changes. Rather than diving over rocks and logs, your hunt comes in the form of strategic planning and orchestration. You are the puller of the strings—the puppeteer—while other, newer pooches do the physical chasing. You are still very much in the chase, but your quarry is much bigger and much wiser.

People have a difficult time moving to what Robert Kiyosaki's rich dad calls the "B" or business quadrant, for two reasons:

1. First, because they either refuse to learn to sell or because they have not honed their sales skills. If you cannot sell, you cannot create or run a successful business. You have to sell to your customers, you have to sell your vision to your staff, to investors and associates. You have to sell yourself daily on why you are taking these risks. Unfortunately there is great talent that gets wasted because there are those who consider sales "dirty." Some would rather sit in secure positions and be bored than put themselves on the firing line that SalesDogs know so well. In fact, my experience has shown me that behind their distaste for selling is a deep-seated fear of being rejected or of failing. Whether you start a business or not, acknowledging that you do in fact sell and you must learn to do it well will transform your life.

2. They cannot or will not put together a team. You have got to be able to gather others who have more skill than you in specific areas. You have got to have enough confidence that your idea or business will

work so as to entice others to come on board. And you have to be committed enough to not abandon the team just because the going gets tough. Seasoned SalesDogs have faced many objections and obstacles. They have put their souls on the line and have battled through good and bad times. They have also built enough confidence to know that they can succeed. Many stay stuck in the S quadrant because they are afraid that they will not make it and thus let everyone else down. They figure that if they are unsuccessful at least they will not feel responsible for others. Mature SalesDogs know how to hold a pack together and how to keep the team going, even in difficult times. They know that there is no way to win the Iditarod with one dog. There is also no way to amass the wealth and income of a successful business with one dog alone.

18

Dogs Just "Do It"

There is one major reason some dogs can hunt and others cannot. It is probably the biggest reason that some people are or are not successful in life. It all comes down to the dialogue in your mind.

What dialogue, you ask?

It's the dialogue with the little voice that just said, "What dialogue?" That is the little voice. I am not sure how a dog's brain actually functions, but I would guess that in its simple way, there is very little distinction between the conscious mind and the subconscious mind. What does that mean? There is the part of your mind that you consciously use all day long. It calculates, it calibrates, it gets you to speak out loud and to make important decisions every minute, like whether or not to have a second helping of dessert or to take a break and have a cappuccino. I have heard many stories and accounts, but the latest I have heard is that on a day-to-day basis we only use a small part of our brain consciously. For the purposes of this discussion, the rest of your mind is called the "subconscious." I know some of you were thinking "unconscious." I will get to that in a minute.

For the purposes of this discussion, when you have that conversation with the little voice in your head, much of its origin comes from the subconscious. You know—the place where your memories of victory and defeat lie semidormant. I do not know if dogs walk around with a little voice chirping away in their heads, or if they debate with it like humans do. You know the conversation I mean—conscious voice (CV) says: "I am going to approach five new prospects today." Little Voice (LV): "What if they don't like me?" CV: "I am going to do it anyway." LV: "You could really get a bit more paperwork done today and go see those prospects tomorrow." You know the routine.

Most people are "unconscious." That means that the little voice that comes from the fears and considerations of their subconscious past and the logical conscious voice of the present appear to be the same. They believe everything that the little voice says to them, good and bad. To them the little voice is reality! They never take a moment to challenge the validity of the little voice's message and simply don't think. These are the people that operate on automatic pilot. When they are faced with an opportunity to grow, seize an opportunity or challenge themselves, the little voice starts blabbing away and they find every reason to avoid responsibility and possible discomfort.

The use or misuse of the little voice is critical to understand. While we have referred to it many times in this book, the simplest way to understand it is in the following cycle.

Great SalesDogs have a very simple cycle. The FIRST STEP in this cycle is that they *seek an opportunity.* In other words, they actually look for a person to throw a ball. They do not sit in a corner and wait for someone to offer it. When I decided years ago that I wanted to make a lot of money in sales, I decided to

SalesDogs Success Cycle

*"I see an opportunity,
I sense there is an opportunity"*

Seek Opportunities

All Create More

Requires Talent & Repetition

Requires Training

More Learning

Feedback

Reciprocated Efforts by Others

More Money

Happy Customers

Celebrate All Wins!

Enablement

*"I can, I have the ability,
I have the resources,
I can try..."*

Barrier to Override

*"I can't. I'm too busy.
I'll do it later.
I have no time."*

Requires Conditioning

Ownership

"I will do it, I am doing it"

** As you cross the Barrier the cycle accelerates
and gains its own momentum.*

ask my manager if I could open a new territory. If I had waited, I might still be waiting. Great SalesDogs do not wait for someone to give them a bone, offer them a promotion and give them a gift. They are actively seeking those treats. Sooner or later they dig one up. I dug up the Hawaiian Islands of Maui and Big Island as my "new" territory. Not bad! By the way, the more you look for opportunities, the better you are at recognizing them. After a year of sales I began to notice patterns in the use of accounting machines, the size of companies that tended to purchase them and their patterns of usage. Many others had traveled to those locations but never had "seen" the opportunity. I made it the number-one territory in the region.

The SECOND STEP is the part called "ENABLEMENT." That means that once the dog sees the person tossing the ball up and down, the little voice says, "I can get this person to toss it for me." Or for us humans, it says, "I am able, I have the resources, I can figure out how to do this." Michael Dell saw a market in made-to-order, direct-sell computer systems and said, "I can do this from my dormitory room," while he was in college.

A friend of mine here in Tahoe did earth-moving for contractors and building sites all spring and summer, and then did carpentry work during the heavy snowfall winters. He saw that the city and county and businesses were paying lots of money for snow removal and were not happy with the service. He said, "I have this equipment just sitting here idle, I can use it to plow the snow." He signed up some very hot contracts at some very win/win rates, employed his same operators to drive the equipment, and he skis all winter.

The THIRD and most crucial step is the OWNERSHIP stage that says, "I am going to do it. I will do it. I am doing it!" The dog goes up to the possessor of the ball and starts its pestering routine. Michael Dell sends out the first advertising fli-

er. I move to the Big Island. My friend walks into the city office of South Lake Tahoe. The Little Voice simply says, "I WILL
DO IT."

If this works, then money comes in, customers get happy,
they refer others, more money flows in and more opportunities
present themselves and the cycle repeats itself with more
speed, momentum and reward.

Simple, right? WRONG! Because most people falter between the "I can" and "I will do it" stage. The Little Voice
sometimes wins and says, "I could go make that call today, but
I won't because I am not feeling up to par today and I would
probably blow it." "I see that I could approach a new market
with our new services, and I know how to do it, but I will try
it next month." "I can make one more sales call today, but I
have some other stuff to do, so I will get to it tomorrow."
Sound familiar?

I do not think dogs go through all this mental anguish,
they just see the opportunity and jump from "I see" to "I will"
to "I did." Great SalesDogs are champions at crossing that line
to "I am doing it." Why do you think that Nike made so much
money with its famous ad campaign that says, "Just do it"? It
is because Nike knows that most people do NOT DO IT! They
talk a good story and come up to the line and find some other
pseudological reason to not do it, or to postpone it, or to pro-
crastinate, even though they know they should "do it." Therefore, if they buy Michael Jordan's shoes, they somehow can
feel like they "did it."

This is the critical piece as to why some dogs can hunt and
some cannot. It is the core of success and personal development. Forget sales for a moment and think about your life. "I
see that there is a fund that has been making a steady gain for
the last three years." "I **am able** to automatically deposit one
hundred dollars per month into it for long-term investing."

"But I **can't** because I do not have enough to even pay my bills," or, "I see that my wife has had a tough day. She looks frazzled. I could take five minutes and just spend the time to hear how she is doing and offer some support . . . but I am too tired, or too busy or I will do it later," or worse yet, "When was the last time she did that for me?"

Each time you back off that line, the distance between you and what you are trying to ultimately achieve, whether it is a sale, wealth or a great relationship, becomes greater and greater. There develops a wall between you and your goals that gets thicker and thicker until after a while dynamite could not blow a hole through it.

The beauty of sales is that it offers daily and moment-to-moment opportunities to cross that line. The great part is that the more you are able to cross that line, regardless of the little voice considerations, the easier it becomes in all areas of your life. It is like the chipping away of an iceberg. Sooner or later there develops a crack that ultimately splits the ice, and a whole series of great things happen. That is how the rich get richer, how great relationships get better over time, and how a SalesDog becomes a champion and the sales start to roll.

The purpose of drilling objections and making calls is not to make sales, but to train and condition your mind to cross the line from "I can" to "I will" to "I did."

One of my clients is Singapore Airlines. It is recognized as possibly one of the top customer-service airlines in the world. This is the same cycle that it developed to transform the customer's experience. Each person in the airline is trained to learn how to cross that line so that when he sees an opportunity to serve a customer, he feels empowered to say, "I can and I will," without having to seek approval or permission. This has catapulted the airline into a realm of service and sales that far exceeds the normal product upgrades that most airlines use to improve sales and service. Each employee and agent is trained to take ownership of the situation and to simply DO the right thing for the customer.

I decided that there was an opportunity in corporate training while I was still in the air cargo business. I knew that I could teach and inspire others to improve their performance and help them improve their lives. Whether I would or not was another story. There was risk and there was a high chance of starving to death.

My wife and I packed our things, left Southern California and headed to Phoenix to begin the new venture. With a deep breath we said, "We will." It was not so hard to do because we had done it before. We had done it in starting the trucking operation, we had done it when we got married, and we had done it each and every day that we faced obstacles in the business, but most important, I had been doing it for years in sales. I moved to the Big Island. I made the extra call each day. I pushed the envelope more times than I should and more times than was prudent, but when the time came to make the big jumps, the confidence was higher. There is always fear, but for great athletes, fear is a great motivator, because in their mind they know that to cross the line means greater strength for some future endeavor.

If you get nothing else from this book, please do me one favor. Put the book down, go up to the significant other person in your life, your kids or the person who is most important to you and seize an opportunity to connect with them. Just say to yourself, "I see an opportunity to take sixty seconds to put something good into this relationship and I can and I will," and just do it! It is the most important step you can take. Do it again and it will become easier. Two things will happen. Your relationship will grow exponentially better. And your ability to cross the line in other areas of your life will jump as well. You will find it easier to sell, easier to make calls, easier to take on new skills, easier to become the person you want to be.

Dogs don't think about it. They look across the room, see you as an opportunity for some companionship and simply walk over and nuzzle their sloppy face into your lap. Try it—it might work!

19

So What Kind of SalesDog Are You Anyway?

S o what kind of SalesDog are you?

Are you the tenacious Pit Bull, who needs only the slightest provocation to jump into the chase?

Are you the more sophisticated Poodle, who understands the critical importance of the first impression, personal marketing and forming relationships with the "right" people?

Are you the Retriever, who never hustles the prospect but "nuzzles" him and serves him at every opportunity until you become the supplier of choice?

Or are you the naturally inquisitive Chihuahua, who loves nothing more than becoming the recognized expert on each and every product in your range? Do you want to be seen as the "font of all knowledge"?

Are you the Basset Hound, who pushes on at your own pace, stays on the scent and establishes credibility and personal rapport over time? Could it be that you are the "Columbo" of the canine family, lulling your prospects into a false sense of comfort and security? Slowly but surely chipping away at their resolve, tracking them to the ends of the earth while the others have given up long ago?

Or perhaps you are a high-rolling Big Dog, who lives for that one big showdown for the big bucks? Or maybe you fantasize about becoming a Big Dog?

Most likely you have recognized a number of characteristics and traits from perhaps a couple of the breeds. You are the ultimate SuperMutt—the most potent and effective pooch in the pound. Perhaps you are a cross-breed mix of several, or on any given day you may exhibit a bit of each.

I hope that this book has brought you to a better understanding of yourself and your strengths. I hope that it has brought you to a place of relative peace where you accept who you are for what you are and stop beating yourself up for all the things that perhaps you are not. One of the myths of sales is that we all have to be perfect, rounded droids in order to be successful. That we all have to be aggressive and ferocious attack dogs to make it big. I hope those myths have been blown. The truth is you just have to know your strengths, play to them and avoid or compensate for your weaknesses. Learn other traits from some of the other SalesDogs and become the ultimate SuperMutt!

I have seen many great SalesDogs throughout my life and throughout the world. They are extremely diverse, and each is phenomenally successful in his or her own unique way. I know that if the breeds are left to run where they feel the most comfortable and happiest they will create incredible results and will continue to thrive and achieve. But even the most exceptional pooch will underperform if you put him in the wrong place.

One of my mentors is David. He is the founder of the infomercial and responsible for more successful direct-marketing campaigns than anyone in America and probably the world. He was born with canine in his blood. Here is how he assessed himself:

David, what breed of DOG would best describe you and why?

My immediate response is a Pit Bull. I'm tenacious, and that's the quality that I know separates me from the pack. If I want to speak to Bill Clinton—I will speak to Bill Clinton. I will make two hundred calls to find someone who knows someone who knows someone who can get him on the phone with me. So the quick response would be Pit Bull.

. . . However, there is no elegance to a Pit Bull. He attacks, I don't attack. He bites hard and clamps down—I don't do either. He's thrilled to leave his adversary wounded or dead—I never do that, knowing I must deal with them another day. He growls and threatens—my forty-plus years of experience has taught me that growling and threatening never work. I like to leave my adversary thinking he got the "best deal in town"—the Pit Bull just doesn't give a damn.

So I would need to add some elegance. Of course, when I think of elegance I think of the Afghan. But there are several problems with my image of an Afghan. First of all they are just about the stupidest animal on four feet. I may not be the brightest, but I know I'm not the stupidest. Second—they require an awful lot of care and attention. I require almost none. And lastly, they're prissy and I'm not prissy.

There is something elegant about the Doberman. My wife Jean has an incredible Doberman that I have lived with for many years. The Doberman is someone like me—aggressive, very smart, low-maintenance.

On the other hand they are feared. People cross the street when they see one—people call me every other day wanting to do "deals" with me. No one wants to do a deal with a Doberman. But I like the subtle mix of fear and respect that the Doberman instills.

Then there is the English Mastiff. I have had four all my life so I am fairly prejudiced, but the Mastiff is also somewhat like me. Big and sloppy, easy maintenance, very loyal and very, very tenacious. They're frightening at first sight but once you get to know them you get to love them. Whenever you're with them you need a "slop rag," since they drool over you—and you have to accept that as part of their being (somewhat like taking the bad with the good).

So bottom line: the English Mastiff (not to be confused with the Bull Mastiff, which is a much smaller, very bitchy dog).

What are the two most important attributes needed to be great in sales?

This question is much easier.

One, always put yourself in the client's shoes. Say to yourself, "If I were this prospect, why would I want to do business with ME?" Think about which elements of the prospect's job he probably hates doing and would love to offload. If you can find that button and press it you can basically put words in his mouth. Learn to think like the prospect, serve the prospect and make his life easier and you will be a hit in sales.

When David pitched me, he simply said, "If I can do xyz for you, would you be willing to pay x percent?" I said, "If you can do that, you have a deal!" Simple as that!

"Give them whatever they want!"

The second thing is communications. When you go to the airport to catch the 9:00 A.M. flight and find out it was canceled at 11:00 the previous night, you go nuts. "Why didn't you call me? I could have made alternative arrangements." When you promise somebody some information on Tuesday, and you can't give it to him—call him as soon as you know and say: "Blair, I can't get you the information today as promised, you'll have it Wednesday by 11:00 A.M. I will call you with the data and send you a confirming fax—if you're not going to be in your office, I'll e-mail it to you so you can get it anywhere." Call people back, always. Call people back promptly. Anticipate your customer's needs and call him with it before he asks. When you complete a job, call the client and tell him so—don't wait for him to call you for a status report. Communicate with him constantly.

True Hound values with the sense of the Retriever.

You asked for two things. Here's my third. Take 1000 percent responsibility. No "It's lost on the truck" excuses. No "It's taking longer than I expected" excuses. No "My bookkeeper didn't come in today" excuses. No excuses. If you screw up—face up to the responsibility. "Hello Blair—I promised to FedEx a brochure to you yesterday, it didn't go out, I'm sorry, I'm sending it today—please accept my apologies—I screwed up."

That's it, my friend.

A true Master.

Of the other myths we uncovered at the start I hope you can see the value of the SalesDog mindset even if you don't work in the field. The truth is we all sell or negotiate all the time. Not everyone is a practicing SalesDog. You may have mentally decided that sales is not your cup of tea, you may work in a field that you don't think relates to sales and for those reasons your natural canine qualities may be lying dormant.

However, even to know your own characteristics for everyday communication is vital for success in all you do. We as human beings assume that people are always like us. For example, if you are a manager you may be reluctant to delegate a particular job because you think it is an awful job. The fact is what is awful for you may be someone else's cup of tea. So being able to recognize the breed of people around you is valuable for much more than just sales. What kind of pooch are you married to? What about your friends? How about your boss? Knowing the behavior and characteristics of those around you will help you to communicate more effectively and live more harmoniously together.

You don't have to have the skin of a rhinoceros and the killer instinct of a tigress on the hunt to survive and thrive in this business. Nor do you need to be that kind of person to get what you want out of life. You can be who you are and be as successful as you want to be as long as you are true to yourself, understand your instinctive talents and strengths and learn to control your mind and your emotions.

I believe there are few more challenging professions than those that offer you the opportunity to influence, convince or sell to others. Where else are you forced to look at yourself and who you really are and what you are really made of every single day? Brilliant salespeople are everywhere. Some are on the front line and some are still somewhat dormant. I would guess that you yourself, in the right situation, could be a relentless hound. They are the great change agents, movers and shakers of society.

As a SalesDog, you must sometimes face rejection, disappointment and disillusionment. You also experience the highs of life, the excitement, the passion and the thrill of success. It is a life that is rarely in balance, yet offers the chance to be the best that you can be every moment.

A dog never gives up. They are enthusiastic and optimistic to the end. That is why the SalesDog was born. We all have the ability to face our own fear, we all have the ability to sell, we all have the ability to achieve our greatest wish, we all have the spirit for the chase and the ability to be optimistic about our chances.

Whether it is your sales staff, your employees, your partners or your children, they all love to win. Your job is to bring out the best in yourself so that you can in turn bring out the best in them and give them a taste of winning. It is already there. If it is spontaneously exciting for you to do this, you will graduate to pack leader and inspire a cast of many. You will win and your pack will win. You will touch the lives of thousands of people whom you will **never** even meet. Their lives and their businesses will be better because of your effort.

Also remember that "Every Dog Has Its Day." Sooner or later that day will come and success will prevail. Be sure to leverage it and build on it—celebrate it and enjoy it.

As humans, we remember mostly things that we see. When we recognize a smile, it is a sign of approval. When we see a familiar face, we remember a friend. But dogs remember what they smell. Once the scent of a deal becomes familiar in their senses, they will be able to track it down from miles away. The scent of the hunt is the same. Trust your sense of smell and teach your SalesDogs to do the same.

Become the master of your own emotions and you will enjoy the freedom, control and power of knowing that you are in the driver's seat of your own life and that no one can ever take that away from you.

Last Word of Advice

As the debate rages on—"Are great salespeople made or born?"—I ask you to decide for yourself. Only you can make that decision. We have extraordinary potential to be whatever we dream to be and it is my genuine wish that this book has, if nothing else, opened that window of possibility in your mind so that you can see that simple truth. They say that "a dog is a man's best friend." As you take your own journey into, out of or around the world of sales, remember the most important rule of all: When the going gets tough, and it will get tough, remember to *be your own best friend. Treat yourself well . . . you deserve it.* Good Hunting and Good Selling!

©EINSTEIN

CASHFLOW® TECHNOLOGIES, INC.

CASHFLOW® Technologies, Inc., and richdad.com, the collaborative efforts of Robert and Kim Kiyosaki and Sharon Lechter, produce innovative financial education products.

The Company's mission Statement is
"To elevate the financial well-being of humanity."

CASHFLOW® Technologies, Inc., presents Robert's teaching through books: *Rich Dad Poor Dad*™, *Rich Dad's CASHFLOW® Quadrant*™, *Rich Dad's Guide to Investing*™, and *Rich Kid Smart Kid*™; board games *CASHFLOW® 101*, *CASHFLOW® 202*, and *CASHFLOW for Kids®*; and tape sets. Additional products are available and under development for people searching for financial education to guide them on their path to financial freedom. For updated information see richdad.com or contact info@richdad.com.

Rich Dad's ADVISORS™

Rich Dad's Advisors is a collection of books and educational products reflecting the expertise of the professional advisors that *CASHFLOW®* Technologies, Inc., and its principals, Robert and Kim Kiyosaki and Sharon Lechter, use to build their financial freedom. Each advisor is a specialist in their respective areas of the B-I Triangle, the business foundation taught by *CASHFLOW®* Technologies, Inc.

CASHFLOW® TECHNOLOGIES, INC.

CASHFLOW® Technologies, Inc., and richdad.com, the collaborative efforts of Robert and Kim Kiyosaki and Sharon Lechter, produce innovative financial education products.

The Company's mission Statement is
   "To elevate the financial well-being of humanity."

CASHFLOW® Technologies, Inc., presents Robert's teaching through books: *Rich Dad Poor Dad™, Rich Dad's CASHFLOW® Quadrant™, Rich Dad's Guide to Investing™,* and *Rich Kid Smart Kid™*; board games *CASHFLOW® 101, CASHFLOW® 202,* and *CASHFLOW for Kids®*; and tape sets. Additional products are available and under development for people searching for financial education to guide them on their path to financial freedom. For updated information see richdad.com or contact info@richdad.com.

Rich Dad's ADVISORS™□

Rich Dad's Advisors is a collection of books and educational products reflecting the expertise of the professional advisors that *CASHFLOW®* Technologies, Inc., and its principals, Robert and Kim Kiyosaki and Sharon Lechter, use to build their financial freedom. Each advisor is a specialist in their respective areas of the B-I Triangle, the business foundation taught by *CASHFLOW®* Technologies, Inc.

<u>*FREE*</u> *OFFER* !!

Get Free Reports on:

- *<u>Fourteen Secrets</u> to multiply your sales and personal cash flow immediately, that I guarantee they did not teach at any sales training course!*

- *For Sales Managers Only: The <u>Missing Link</u> on how to reverse the old 80/20 rule of sales!*

To get them, just go to our Web site at:

SalesDogs.com

And also discover the answer to:

What Kind of a SalesDog are You?

By taking the SalesDog Diagnostic, you will find out what type of salesperson (SalesDog) you are so that you can use your hidden talents to <u>sell tons more</u> immediately!

Plus…
More SalesDogs tool kits and programs that will make your life ten times easier!

<u>Contact us in the USA at:</u>
SalesDogs
P.O. Box 10373
Zephyr Cove, NV 89448 USA
<u>Toll Free in US</u> (877) 337-1700
Direct: (775) 589-1911
Fax: (775) 588-2611

<u>In Australia:</u>
Pow Wow Events
4-6 Mentmore Avenue Rosebury NSW 2108
P.O. Box 122 Rosebery NSW 1445

Phone: 61-2-9662-8488
Fax: 61-2-9662-8611

Three Different Games
CASHFLOW, Investing 101®:

CASHFLOW® *101* teaches you the basics of fundamental investing, but it also does much more. *CASHFLOW*® *101* teaches you how to take control of your personal finances, build a business through proper cash flow management, and learn how to invest with greater confidence in real estate and other businesses.

This educational product is for you if you want to improve your business and investing skills by learning how to take your ideas and turn them into assets such as your own business. Many small businesses fail because the owner lacks capital, real-life experience, and basic accounting skills. Many people think investing is risky simply because they cannot read financial statements. *CASHFLOW*® *101* teaches the fundamental skills of financial literacy and investing. This educational product includes the board game, a video, and audiotapes. It takes approximately two complete times playing the game to understand it. Then we recommend that you play the game at least six times to begin to master the fundamentals of cash flow management and investing.
Price $195 U.S.

CASHFLOW, Investing 202®:

CASHFLOW® 202 teaches you the advanced skills of technical investing. After you are comfortable with the fundamentals of CASHFLOW® 101, the next educational challenge is learning how to manage the ups and down of the market, often called volatility. CASHFLOW® 202 uses the same board game as 101, but it comes with a completely different set of cards and score sheets and more advanced audiotapes. CASHFLOW® 202 teaches you to use the investment techniques of qualified investors— techniques such as short selling, call options, put options, and straddles—that can be very expensive to learn in the real market. Most investors are afraid of a market crash. A qualified investor uses the tools taught in CASHFLOW® 202 to make money when the markets go up and when the markets come down.

After you have mastered 101, CASHFLOW® 202 becomes very exciting because you learn to react to the highs and lows of the market, and you make a lot of paper money. Again, it is a lot less expensive to learn these advanced trading techniques on a board game using paper money than trading in the market with real money. While these games cannot guarantee your investment success, they will improve your financial vocabulary and knowledge of these advanced investing techniques.
Price $95 U.S.

CASHFLOW, Investing for Kids®:

Could your child be the next Bill Gates, Anita Roddick of the Body Shop, Warren Buffet, or Donald Trump? If so, then CASHFLOW for Kids® could be the family's educational and fun game that gives your child the same educational head start my rich dad gave me. Few people know that Warren Buffet's father was a stockbroker and Donald Trump's father was a real estate developer. A parent's influence at an early age can have long-term financial results. CASHFLOW for Kids® includes the board game, book, and audiotape.
Price $59.95 U.S.

Robert Kiyosaki's Edumercial
An Educational Commercial

The Three Incomes

In the world of accounting, there are three different types of income: earned, passive, and portfolio. When my real dad said to me, "Go to school, get good grades, and find a safe secure job," he was recommending I work for earned income. When my rich dad said, "The rich don't work for money, they have their money work for them," he was talking about passive income and portfolio income. Passive income, in most cases, is derived from real estate investments. Portfolio income is income derived from paper assets such as stocks, bonds, and mutual funds.

Rich dad used to say, "The key to becoming wealthy is the ability to convert earned income into passive income and/or portfolio income as quickly as possible." He would say, "The taxes are highest on earned income. The least taxed income is passive income. That is another reason why you want your money working hard for you. The government taxes the income you work hard for more than the income your money works hard for."

The Key to Financial Freedom

The key to financial freedom and great wealth is a person's ability or skill to convert earned income into passive income and/or portfolio income. That is the skill that my rich dad spent a lot of time teaching Mike and me. Having that skill is the reason my wife, Kim, and I are financially free, never needing to work again. We continue to work because we choose to. Today we own a real estate investment company for passive income and participate in private placements and initial public offerings of stock for portfolio income.

Investing to become rich requires a different set of personal skills, skills essential for financial success as well as low-risk and high-investment returns. In other words, the knowledge to create assets that buy other assets. The problem is that gaining the basic education and experience required is often time consuming, frightening, and expensive, especially when you make mistakes with your own money. That is why I created my patented educational board games, trademarked as CASHFLOW.

Please visit our Web site,
www.richdad.com
to review:

- Additional Information About Our Financial Education Products
- Frequently Asked Questions (FAQs) About Our Products
- Seminars, Events, and Appearances with Robert Kiyosaki

Thank You